Edexcel GCSE

Business:
Introduction to Small Business

Student Book

Alain Anderton • Ian Gunn
Andrew Ashwin consultant editor

edexcel

A PEARSON COMPANY

Acknowledgements

Pearson Education Limited
Edinburgh Gate
Harlow
Essex
CM 20 2JE
England
© Pearson Education 2009

ISBN 978-1-84690-496-7

15 14 13 12
10 9 8 7 6

Graphics by Kevin O'Brien
Cartoons by Alan Fraser
Photography Andrew Allen
Edited by Dave Gray
Proof reading by Mike Kidson
Cover image by © Getty Images/Martin Mistretta

First edition 2009
Page origination by Caroline Waring-Collins, Waring Collins Ltd
Printed and bound by Scotprint, Haddington, Scotland

The publisher and author wish to thank the following for materials and photographs used in the production of this book.
BBC p96, Digital Vision pp 95, 123, Photodisk p 59, Michael Simon/Rex Features p 93 (r), Shutterstock pp 6, 7, 8, 10, 11, 15, 16, 17, 19, 20, 21, 23, 24, 25, 27, 34, 35, 36, 39, 43, 44, 45, 47, 48, 50, 51, 52, 54, 55, 56, 58, 62, 63, 64, 64, 65, 66, 67, 68, 69, 71, 72, 76, 77, 79, 80, 80, 81, 82, 83, 84, 90, 91, 92, 99, 100, 103, 104, 105, 107108, 109, 111, 114, 115, 116, 118,119, 120, 124, 126, 127, 128, 129, 131, 132, 135, 138-151, 152, 158. Stockbyte pp 38, 40, 122, Topfoto p98.

Thanks
I would like to thank Dave Gray, who as usual has done a superb job publishing and editing the book, Mike Kidson for proof reading and Andrew Ashwin, who has given invaluable feedback. The page origination was sensitively accomplished by Caroline Waring-Collins. Not least I would like to thank my wife for her help with the project.
Alain Anderton

My wife Mary for her long suffering patience, support and encouragement, the 6953 Dream Team for their inspiration. Per magistra, ave Maria. Ian Gunn

I would like to thank all my colleagues at Biz/ed for supporting me in doing this project, specifically Andy Hargrave, Jill Jones, Stewart Perrygrove and John Yates. There are many people who worked on the development of the qualification on which this book is based. Their faith, support, encouragement and considerable hard work and skill were crucial in getting the qualification live. As a result thanks go to Susan Hoxley, Kelly Padwick, Beverley Anim-Antwi, Derek Richardson and Lizzie Firth. No book would be produced without the dedication of the authors who combine considerable work pressures with the task of producing the book and supporting materials, mostly in their own time. The fact that the production process has been relatively trouble free is largely due to their dedication, commitment, professionalism and support. Thanks go to Alain Anderton, Ian Gunn, Keith Hirst, Andrew Malcolm, Jonathan Shields and Nicola Walker for their contributions and effort. At Pearson, Dave Gray has been a much valued publisher - his skill in handling people, deadlines, vast quantities of text and queries, whilst retaining patience and humour, has been invaluable. It has been a privilege to work with you Dave - thank you. Finally, thanks go to my family, Sue, Alex and Johnny for their patience and love. Andrew Ashwin

Contents: delivering the EDEXCEL GCSE Business (Introduction to Small Business) Specification Unit 1

Welcome to the Edexcel GCSE Business Studies series

The Edexcel GCSE Business Studies Series has been produced to build students' business knowledge, understanding and skills, and to help them prepare for their GCSE assessment. The books include lots of engaging features to enthuse students and provide the range of support needed. The student books in the series are:

- **Introduction to Small Business** covering Units 1 and 2 (compulsory for the Full Course) and Unit 6 (for the Short Course)
- **Building a business** (Unit 3)
- **Business Communications** (Unit 4)
- **Introduction to Economic Understanding** (Unit 5)

Introduction to Small Business

Unit 1: The specification emphasises small businesses and business start-ups and the book reflects this focus. Every example and case study relates to a small business context rather than large organisations that are often difficult to understand. The text helps build understanding and confidence in what many are interested in – how to set up and run a small business. The sums of money involved are not bewildering and abstract and the subject feels very real.

Unit 2: This is the controlled assessment Unit for the core part of the qualifi0cation. Controlled assessment is new to the course and so presents its own challenges. The advice given will help to make sense of its aims and purpose, and there is plenty of practical advice on how to research and write up the work.

Unit 6: The content, questions and guidance for Units 1 and 2 cover Unit 6 (the Short Course).

How to use this book

Each Edexcel GCSE Business Studies unit is divided into topics. These books are written in the same easy-to-follow format, with each topic split into digestible chapters. You will find these features in each chapter:

Topic overview A case study sets the scene for each topic, accompanied by a series of questions. Your teacher might look at this as a starter activity to find out what you already know about the subject. You'll find a summary of the assessment for the topic.

Content and objectives Each chapter starts with a case study to put the content in a context, followed by the objectives for that chapter.

Edexcel key terms are highlighted and defined in each chapter.

Test yourself question practice in every chapter contains objective and multiple choice questions.

Over to you question practice in every chapter. A short case study is followed by questions written in exam paper style.

Annotated sample students' answer and revisions support to help students prepare for the exams.

We've broken down the six stages of revision to ensure you are prepared every step of the way.

Zone in: How to get into the perfect 'zone' for revision.

Planning zone: Tips and advice on how to effectively plan revision.

Know zone: The facts you need to know, memory tips and exam-style practice at the end of every topic.

Don't panic zone: Last-minute revision tips.

Exam zone: What to expect on the exam paper and the key terms used.

Zone out: What happens after the exams.

ResultsPlus

These features use exam performance data to help you prepare as well as you can.

There are three different types of ResultsPlus features throughout this book:

Exam question reports show previous exam questions with details about how well students answered them.

- Red shows the number of students who scored low marks
- Orange shows the number of students who did okay
- Green shows the number of students who did well.

They explain how students could have achieved the top marks so that you can make sure that you answer these questions correctly in future.

ResultsPlus
Exam Question Report

(b) (ii) Identify **one** type of desk research. **(1)** (June 2006)

How students answered

Many students (44%) answered this question incorrectly (0 marks). The main reason was a lack of understanding of the difference between desk (secondary) and field (primary) research. As a result, some gave examples of field research, such as market research/taking a sample of customers' views/using questionnaires.

The majority of students (56%) answered this question correctly (1 mark). Common correct answers given included government statistics/specialist articles/Internet/existing market research reports/existing sales figures.

ResultsPlus
Watch Out!

Small businesses have very limited resources for researching their market. Many small business start-ups do very little market research. They rely on the gut instinct of the person setting up the business. But a start-up business which has done some market research is more likely to survive and be successful than a start-up business which has done very little market research. Market research can help to reduce the risk involved even if it is only by a small amount.

Watch out! These warn you about common mistakes and misconceptions that students often make.

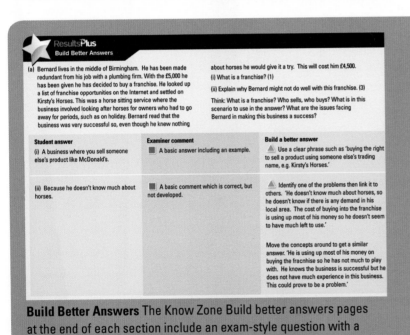

ResultsPlus
Build Better Answers

(a) Bernard lives in the middle of Birmingham. He has been made redundant from his job with a plumbing firm. With the £5,000 he has been given he has decided to buy a franchise. He looked up a list of franchise opportunities on the Internet and settled on Kirsty's Horses. This was a horse sitting service where the business involved looking after horses for owners who had to go away for periods, such as on holiday. Bernard read that the business was very successful so, even though he knew nothing about horses he would give it a try. This will cost him £4,500.

(i) What is a franchise? (1)

(ii) Explain why Bernard might not do well with this franchise. (3)

Think: What is a franchise? Who sells, who buys? What is in this scenario to use in the answer? What are the issues facing Bernard in making this business a success?

Student answer	Examiner comment	Build a better answer
(i) A business where you sell someone else's product like McDonald's.	■ A basic answer including an example.	⚠ Use a clear phrase such as 'buying the right to sell a product using someone else's trading name, e.g. Kirsty's Horses.'
(ii) Because he doesn't know much about horses.	■ A basic comment which is correct, but not developed.	⚠ Identify one of the problems then link it to others. 'He doesn't know much about horses, so he doesn't know if there is any demand in his local area. The cost of buying into the franchise is using up most of his money so he doesn't seem to have much left to use.' Move the concepts around to get a similar answer. 'He is using up most of his money on buying the frachnise so he has not much to play with. He knows the business is successful but he does not have much experience in this business. This could prove to be a problem.'

Build Better Answers The Know Zone Build better answers pages at the end of each section include an exam-style question with a student answer, examiner comments and an improved answer so that you can improve your own writting.

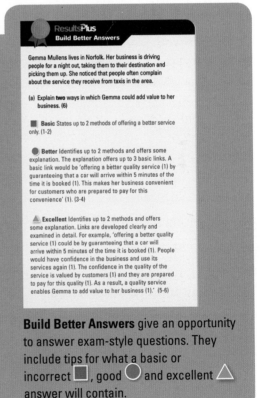

ResultsPlus
Build Better Answers

Gemma Mullens lives in Norfolk. Her business is driving people for a night out, taking them to their destination and picking them up. She noticed that people often complain about the service they receive from taxis in the area.

(a) Explain **two** ways in which Gemma could add value to her business. **(6)**

■ **Basic** States up to 2 methods of offering a better service only. (1-2)

● **Better** Identifies up to 2 methods and offers some explanation. The explanation offers up to 3 basic links. A basic link would be 'offering a better quality service (1) by guaranteeing that a car will arrive within 5 minutes of the time it is booked (1). This makes her business convenient for customers who are prepared to pay for this convenience' (1). (3-4)

▲ **Excellent** Identifies up to 2 methods and offers some explanation. Links are developed clearly and examined in detail. For example, 'offering a better quality service (1) could be by guaranteeing that a car will arrive within 5 minutes of the time it is booked (1). People would have confidence in the business and use its services again (1). The confidence in the quality of the service is valued by customers (1) and they are prepared to pay for this quality (1). As a result, a quality service enables Gemma to add value to her business (1).' (5-6)

Build Better Answers give an opportunity to answer exam-style questions. They include tips for what a basic or incorrect ■, good ○ and excellent △ answer will contain.

Assessment

Information on external examinations is covered in the Examzone at the end of the book. This provides details on assessment for the Unit 1 or Unit 6 exams (see pages 152-162). There is a whole section of valuable information about the Unit 2 controlled assessment, starting on page 138.

Topic 1.1: Spotting a business opportunity

Topic overview

This topic considers how to spot a successful business opportunity. What do customers need and how can this be identified? What gaps in the market are there? What are other businesses doing? How can value be added? Should a business buy into an existing franchise or not?

Case study

Kristen Lockey had worked for her father's building company for ten years. Now, she wanted to go it alone and start her own business. She didn't want to compete directly with her father's company. So she looked around for a different line of business. After much research, she came up with the idea of setting up a business specialising in building conservatories, verandas and decking.

Her father's company had already done a few jobs installing conservatories. Kristen knew that there was a good market out there. However, she didn't want to compete directly with the big companies in the market. They advertised heavily and had large numbers of people in sales, promoting their products. Kristen saw, though, there was a gap in the market for one-off, specially designed conservatories and decking. These would be made with the best materials. So Kristen would be able to charge her customers a high price for a product which had a lot of value added. High quality both of the product and of service would be the unique selling points for the business.

In her research, Kristen looked at whether there were any franchising opportunities available in the manufacture of conservatories. Taking on a franchise could help her establish her own business. However, she couldn't find anything that looked suitable. So she decided that she would have to set up in business on her own.

1. Why are the needs of customers important for the success of Kristen Lockey's new business?

2. Explain why Kristen Lockey decided to make 'one-off, specially designed' conservatories.

3. Why might an entrepreneur looking to set up a new business consider a franchise?

What will I learn?

Understanding customer needs Why are customer needs central to starting a business? What are the different types of market research? How can market research data be collected and interpreted? Why is market knowledge through direct customer contact important?

Market mapping How can customer buying habits and preferences be analysed? How can businesses identify market segments? How can businesses map their market and identify market gaps?

Analysing competitor strengths and weaknesses Why should initial planning for a business start-up include an analysis of market competitors? How can competitor strengths and weaknesses be analysed? Why should a business compare its offering with that its rivals?

Understanding the need to add value What is meant by 'added value' and why is it important to business survival and success? What are the main sources of added value?

What options exist for starting up a business? What is a franchise? What are the advantages and disadvantages of using a franchise to start up a business compared to other alternatives? What is a good location for a business?

How will I be assessed?

Unit 1 A forty-five minute written examination of multiple choice and objective test questions.

Unit 2 Research and investigate a real life business from a choice of five tasks and write up the results under controlled assessment conditions.

Unit 6 A forty-five minute written examination of multiple choice, objective test and extended answer questions.

1 Businesses

Case Study

Jack Padmore has just set up a business renting out bouncy castles. His children loved playing on bouncy castles and he had often hired one for birthday parties. It looked the sort of business he could do too in his spare time to earn some extra money.

Objectives

- Understand what a business does.
- Appreciate that most businesses are very small.
- Appreciate that large numbers of businesses are created and closed down each year.
- Understand the concepts of production, suppliers, customers and markets.
- Appreciate that there are many important aspects to starting up a business.

ResultsPlus
Watch Out!

You often hear about very successful businesses and entrepreneurs making millions of pounds and becoming very wealthy. The number of people who become very wealthy through starting up their own business is small. Also, many people start a business for other reasons than making large amounts of money. For example, they may enjoy working for themselves and being their own boss.

Small businesses

In the UK today, there are over 4 million businesses. This is about one business for every 13 people living in the country. A few of these businesses are large businesses like Tesco, Toyota or British Gas. But there are only around 33,000 businesses that employ more than 50 people. Almost all businesses are therefore small businesses. Three quarters of all businesses have only one person, the owner, working in the business. Jack Padmore's business was a business like this. He was the only person who worked in the business.

New businesses are being created all the time. According to one estimate, 200,000 new businesses are created each year in the UK. Equally, businesses are being closed down all the time. Of the 200,000 new businesses created each year, one in ten will have closed within the first 12 months. One in three will have closed within three years. Less than half will still exist after five years.

The purpose of a business

Why do businesses exist? Why do we need businesses? The answer is that businesses exist to make goods and services.

- Goods are physical items like a can of baked beans, a litre of petrol, a Nintendo Wii or a bus.
- Services are non-physical products like a hair cut, a bus journey, a lesson in a classroom or a consultation with a doctor.

Most businesses make services rather than goods. Around 70 per cent of all that is produced in the UK are services. Nearly 8 in every 10 people work in service industries. The chances are that you too will work in a service industry. Jack Padmore's business is a service business. Businesses that rent out products like bouncy castles provide a service to customers.

Production

Businesses make goods and services. They do this by buying resources such as raw materials, labour and machines and then using them to make products. Jack Padmore, for example, uses a number of different resources in his business.

- There are different pieces of equipment: the bouncy castle itself, an electric pump to blow it up and a van to transport the bouncy castle.
- There are raw materials. He has to put petrol into his van. He also uses electricity to power the electric pump.
- There is also his time (called 'labour'). Workers are very important to any business.

Suppliers and customers

Businesses buy the goods and services they need from **suppliers**, as shown in Figure 1. Jack Padmore, for example, bought his bouncy castle from a bouncy castle manufacturer. The petrol he puts into his van comes from garages.

Businesses sell to **customers**. Most of Jack Padmore's customers are ordinary people who hire a bouncy castle for a special event. They are **consumers** of the product that he sells. Some of Jack Padmore's customers, though, are other businesses. A business might hire a bouncy castle for a works party. Sometimes a local pub will hire a bouncy castle for a weekend for a special event.

Markets

Jack Padmore's business operates in a number of different **markets**. A market exists in any situation when buyers and sellers exchange goods and services. There is a market for bouncy castle hire. It is a part of a larger market for equipment hire for entertainment. When Jack Padmore fills up his van with petrol, he is a small buyer in the large worldwide market for oil. Whenever Jack buys from a supplier or sells to a customer, he is operating within a market.

Setting up in business

When Jack Padmore set up his business, he had a lot of things to think about.
- He had to spot a business opportunity. Would customers hire his bouncy castle?
- There was the finance to think about. Did he have the money to start the business? Could he make a profit out of the business?
- What would he have to buy to get the business up and running?
- There were also the legal aspects to worry about. Health and safety would be very important. He would have to take out insurance in case someone had an accident on his bouncy castle. Then he would have to sort out paying the right amount of tax to the government.

Going out of business

Jack Padmore closed his business after three years. The business was moderately successful and orders came in on a regular basis, particularly during the summer months. But he was not making enough profit to make it worthwhile. It was not just the time he spent travelling to a customer, putting up the bouncy castle and taking it down again. There was all the paper work and the telephone calls. He was doing all this in his spare time. His regular job brought him in enough money for him to be comfortably off. The bouncy castle business added a lot of pressure to his life without bringing in the sort of money that might have made it worthwhile. Jack Padmore became part of the statistic that says more than half of all new businesses do not survive their first five years of operation.

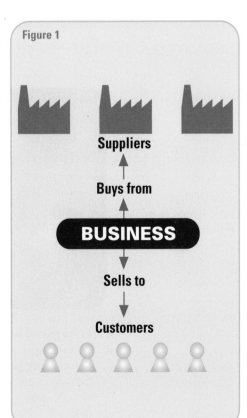

Figure 1

Suppliers

Buys from

BUSINESS

Sells to

Customers

edexcel key terms

Supplier – a business which sells (or supplies) products to another business.

Customer – any person or organisation which buys or is supplied with a product by a business.

Consumer – the person who ultimately uses (or consumes) a product.

Markets – where buyers and sellers meet to exchange goods and services.

10

ResultsPlus
Build Better Answers

Asif Rahman trained as an artist at college. His business paints designs on cars and motor bikes from a workshop. Which **two** of the following business activities would involve him dealing directly with suppliers?

A Ringing a car dealer to say a design is ready

B Paying business rates to the local authority

C Ordering paint for the designs

D Talking to a bike owner about a new design

E Taking delivery of leaflets to advertise the paint shop

F Receiving payment for a design

Answer C and E

Technique guide: There is a number of choices available so first:

Think: What service do suppliers provide for a business? Who are the suppliers to Asif's business?

Then: Dismiss the choices that are obviously wrong – B involves dealing with the local authority which is neither a supplier or a customer.

Decide: You are left with A, C, D, E and F. You have narrowed down the options.

Go through these: A, D and F are all activities that deal directly with customers.

This leaves you with the correct answers of C and E. Suppliers provide services for the business such as providing paint supplies and printing leaflets.

Test yourself

1. What is the purpose of a business? Select **one** answer.

A *To give everyone a job*
B *To make big profits for its owners*
C *To produce goods and services*
D *To pay taxes to the government*

2. A small business makes cakes for parties and weddings. Which **two** of the following are most likely to be resources it uses directly in production? Select **two** of the following.

A *Labour*
B *Taxes*
C *Television adverts*
D *Flour*
E *Airfreight*

3. Justin Terrett is a professional DJ who travels to engagements in his van with all his kit. Which **two** of the following are most likely to be suppliers to his business? Select **two** of the following.

A *A club renting his services*
B *A television company writing an article about the business*
C *A local petrol garage*
D *The individuals who attend his gigs*
E *Record stores*

Over to you

The Jayne Varndall Motorcycle School prepares motorcyclists for their riding tests. To ride a motorcycle, you need to have a specialist driving licence which is different from one for driving a car or a lorry. Jayne Varndall, the owner, employs four people: a secretary and administrator and three instructors. She has an office and a large car park that she uses to instruct motorcyclists at the start of their training. Her business has operated for the past six years.

Jayne's customers pay for a basic instruction course in riding a bike. Then they are charged by the hour for on-road practice before taking their test at a local government centre. For their training, they can either hire a motorbike from her or bring their own bike. The market for motorcycle instruction is competitive. There are three other businesses in the area that offer similar services. There used to be four, but one business closed down because it couldn't get enough customers.

1. 'Jayne Varndall provides a service to her customers.' What is meant by 'a service' and 'customers' for Jayne Varndall's business? (4)

2. Identify and explain how **two** resources are used by Jayne Varndall to produce the service she provides. (8)

3. 'One business closed down because it could not get enough customers'. Giving reasons for your answer, analyse **two** possible reasons why Jayne Varndall's business has managed to survive against the competition for six years. (6)

2 Understanding customer needs

Case Study

Ben Noakes has worked for 15 years for Tesco. He has worked his way up from the bottom doing a variety of jobs. Now he wants to do something else apart from work for a big firm. Ben wants to set up his own business. Because the only thing he knows about is retailing (shops), Ben has begun to investigate setting up his own shop. He thinks he might have spotted the right business opportunity - a fancy dress shop.

Objectives

● Understand that customer needs are central to starting a business.

● Understand how to collect and interpret primary and secondary market research in the context of starting a new business.

● Understand the difference between qualitative and quantitative research data.

● Understand the value of market knowledge through direct customer contact.

edexcel ::: key terms

Customer needs – the wants and desires of buyers of a product or the customers of a business.

Market research – the process of gaining information about customers, competitors and market trends through collecting primary and secondary data.

Primary (or field) research – the gathering of new information, called primary data, which has not been collected before.

Customer needs

Working for Tesco has taught Ben that putting customers first is essential for the success of a business. Tesco today is the UK's largest retailer. £1 in every £8 that the British consumer spends in shops is spent at Tesco. One of the reasons why Tesco is so successful is that it gives its shoppers what they want to buy, at the right price and in the right place.

Ben has always enjoyed fancy dress parties. But there is no fancy dress shop in the large town that he lives in now. Hiring a fancy dress costume means a thirty minute car ride to the next town. His **customer needs** are definitely not being met here.

When he goes into a fancy dress shop, Ben wants plenty of choice at a reasonable price. The costumes should be well made and in good condition. There is nothing more annoying that hiring an outfit and finding the zip is broken, there are buttons missing or there is a tear in the fabric. Ben also appreciates knowledgeable and friendly service. Going to choose a costume is part of the fun of going to a fancy dress party.

Ben thinks that his customers have the same needs as he does:

• convenient location;
• reasonable price;
• good range;
• good quality;
• knowledgeable and friendly customer service.

Market research

Leaving his job and setting up on his own is a big step for Ben. Whilst he might think a fancy dress shop is a good idea, others might not think the same way. To make his business a success, he needs plenty of customers.

To make sure that he is doing the right thing, Ben has been conducting some **market research**. This is designed to give information about his likely market, such as who his customers might be and what they might be prepared to pay for purchases. There are two types of market research: primary research and secondary research.

Primary research

Primary research (or **field research**) involves the collection of **primary data** - information which no one else has collected. There are several types of primary research.

- **Surveys** usually involve asking questions of **respondents** – people or organisations who reply to the questions asked. The list of questions asked is called a **questionnaire**. You might have seen people in the local high street with clip boards asking people to answer a questionnaire. Surveys can also be conducted over the telephone. A business might conduct a survey of the views of its workers.
- A **focus group** is a small group of people. They are invited by the researcher to talk together about a product or idea. The researcher then records their responses. With a focus group, the researcher is particularly interested in how people react to each other as they talk. This can point to whether a product or idea will be successful or not.
- **Observation** is another type of primary research. Looking at and recording how people or other businesses behave can give important information.
- In some situations it is possible to conduct **experiments**. For example, a small manufacturing business might build a number of early versions (called 'prototypes') of a new product. It could show these prototypes to potential customers to see their reaction.

Ben Noakes used three of these types of market research. Firstly, he conducted a survey of his friends, his work colleagues and anybody else he could get to answer his questions. He wanted to know

- whether they had ever hired or bought fancy dress costumes;
- what sort of costumes did they wear to parties;
- how much were they prepared to pay;
- from where did they get costumes.

He also noted down some personal details like whether they were male or female, approximate age and whether they had young children. The answers to these questions gave him some guide as to what his sales might be and what he should offer for sale in his shop.

The second type of market research he used was observation. When he went to fancy dress parties, he jotted down what everyone was wearing. More importantly, he visited the nearest ten fancy dress shops he could find. He pretended to be a customer. In fact, he noted down the location of the shop, how the shop was laid out and what stock they seemed to have. He wrote down some sample prices and the conditions of sale for hire of costumes. He also tried to assess how friendly the staff were.

Third, he invited some friends round to dinner. He then used them as a focus group. By introducing ideas about how he would run his future business, he could see their reactions.

Primary research, using a questionnaire

ResultsPlus
Watch Out!

Researchers must be very careful about bias when conducting surveys. How questions are worded can affect the answers that are given. Also, who is asked to answer the survey can be untypical of the target customer. For example, if you conducted a survey of ten of your friends about baked beans, it is most unlikely that the results would be typical of the average buyer of baked beans.

edexcel ::: key terms

Survey – research involving asking questions of people or organisations.

Respondents – those who provide data for a survey usually by answering questions in a questionnaire or interview.

Questionnaire – a list of questions to be answered by respondents, designed to gather information about consumers' tastes.

Focus group – in market research, a group of people brought together to answer questions and discuss a product, brand or issue.

14

Secondary research

Secondary or desk research involves the collection of secondary data. This is information which is already available both from within an existing business and from outside the business.

Ben knew, for example, that Tesco constantly analyses its sales. Products that do not sell well in an individual store are withdrawn and the shelf space used to stock goods that sell better. Once his shop was up and running, Ben would be able to analyse data like sales to decide what to sell.

For the time being, though, Ben had to research using data that came from outside the business.

* One simple piece of data he used was the **telephone directory**. He looked in Yellow Pages and its competitor

ResultsPlus
Watch Out!

Small businesses have very limited resources for researching their market. Many small business start-ups do very little market research. They rely on the gut instinct of the person setting up the business. But a start-up business which has done some market research is more likely to survive and be successful than a start-up business which has done very little market research. Market research can help to reduce the risk involved even if it is only by a small amount.

edexcel ⠿ key terms

Secondary (or desk) research – the process of gathering secondary data, which is information that has already been gathered such as sales records, government statistics, newspaper articles or reports from market research groups.

Qualitative data – information about opinions, judgements and attitudes.

Quantitative data – data that can be expressed as numbers and can be statistically analysed.

Sources of secondary research

Thomson Local Directory to find the location of all the fancy dress shops within a fifty mile radius. He could also see the size of the entry and what made an attractive advertisement in these directories.

* He put 'Fancy Dress Shop UK' into the Google search engine on the **Internet** on his computer. He found hundreds of sites. On some of them, you could order goods over the internet. Others were little more than an advertisement for a shop. He found it interesting to browse through the sites for two reasons. First, he could see what they were selling. Second, he could see the prices they were charging. He also wondered whether he ought to have a website and if so, what would he want it to do.
* Ben looked in the **local newspapers** in his area to see whether any of the existing fancy dress shops advertised in these publications. This would tell him whether or not it would be worthwhile for him to advertise.
* Ben went to a large reference library thirty miles away to see whether there were any **market reports** on Fancy Dress shops. Market reports are produced by market research organisations such as Mintel. At several hundred pounds each, they are too expensive for a small business to buy. But they were available to read for free at the public library.

Qualitative and quantitative data

Some of the information that Ben collected was qualitative data. This is information about opinions, judgements and attitudes. Ben was collecting qualitative data when he asked friends about their likes and dislikes of fancy dress costumes, or of fancy dress shops. He was also collecting qualitative data when he tried to get an impression of the level of customer service when he visited existing fancy dress shops.

Other information collected was quantitative data. This is data that can be interpreted in a numerical way. For example, from his survey, Ben was able to say that 30 per cent of his respondents used a fancy dress shop in one nearby town, 20 per cent used a different fancy dress shop in another town and 50 per cent made their own costumes. He was also able to say what proportion of respondents spent £1-£10, £11-£20, £20-£30 and over £30 on a fancy dress outfit.

Direct customer contact

Tesco is a highly successful retailer because it understands its customers. It has complex computer systems that analyse what customers are buying. Ben knows that, once his business is up and running, he must listen to his customers. These customers will be vital in giving him market knowledge. Direct customer contact will help him to understand how the fancy dress market is working and how it is changing.

Interpreting the data

In his market research, Ben collected a large amount of data. He then had to interpret (or **analyse**) the data. What did it all mean? What was important and what was not important? He analysed the quantitative data, comparing numbers like prices and ages of customers. The qualitative data showed him that what he liked was not necessarily what other people liked. He would have to listen hard to his customers to get the formula for his shop just right.

Overall, though, Ben judged that his market research showed there would be enough customers for his shop to be a success. However, he knew there was a risk that the market research could be wrong. If there were too few customers, his business would fail.

Over to you

Grace and Peter Fletcher had always made fabulous cakes. Their friends knew this and often, when picking up children from school, they would be asked to make a cake for a

child's birthday party. As their children got older, they began to think that they could turn their cake making skills into a proper business.

Grace and Peter took their time to research the market. They had kept records and photographs of all the cakes made for other people. They analysed these to see what sort of cakes were popular and how much they had charged. Going to their local supermarket, they saw what special cakes were available on the shelves. For several Saturdays in a row, they spent an hour in the cake aisle noting down who bought these special cakes. They used the local telephone directory, *Yellow Pages* and *Thomson Local Directory* to see who offered cake making services in the local area. They rang all the local suppliers to get a quote on a cake, so that they could see what prices the potential competition charged. They also looked in their local newspaper to see if cake makers paid for advertisements and what sort of adverts they placed.

During this period of research, when they made a cake for someone else, they would make a second small cake exactly the same. They would invite their friends round for a cup of coffee and a piece of the second cake. This was so they could listen to their opinions about cakes.

1. Explain what is meant by 'primary research'. In your answer, give **two** examples of primary research used by Grace and Peter Fletcher. (6)

2. Explain what is meant by 'secondary research'. In your answer, give **two** examples of secondary research used by Grace and Peter Fletcher. (6)

3. Do you think that Grace and Peter Fletcher have a good understanding of their customers' needs? Justify your answer. (6)

Test yourself

1. Chris wants to set up a business fitting kitchens and looks in Yellow Pages (a commercial telephone directory) to see what other businesses offer similar services in his area. This is an example of what type of research? Select **one** answer.

   A **Qualitative**
   B **Primary**
   C **Secondary**
   D **Observation**

2. Which **one** of the following is a type of primary research? Select **one** answer.

   A **Conducting a survey**
   B **Analysing past sales figures of other businesses**
   C **Reading market reports**
   D **Consulting local newspapers**

3. Which **two** of the following are most likely to give a researcher qualitative data? Select **two** answers.

   A **The meeting of a focus group**
   B **Researching names of businesses in an area from a telephone directory**
   C **Researching the products made by competitors by looking at internet sites**
   D **Conducting interviews with shoppers in a supermarket**
   E **Analysing government statistics**

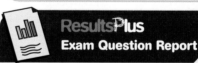

ResultsPlus
Exam Question Report

(b) (ii) Identify **one** type of desk research. (1) (June 2006)
How students answered

Many students (44%) answered this question incorrectly (0 marks). The main reason was a lack of understanding of the difference between desk (secondary) and field (primary) research. As a result, some gave examples of field research, such as market research/taking a sample of customers' views/using questionnaires.

The majority of students (56%) answered this question correctly (1 mark). Common correct answers given included government statistics/specialist articles/Internet/existing market research reports/existing sales figures.

3 Market mapping

Case Study

Ruby Jacobs was just 21 years of age. She came from a family of shopkeepers. Her mother owned a ladies fashion boutique, whilst her uncle owned a general grocery store. Having studied Food and Catering for three years at university, Ruby wanted to set up her own business. She decided that for her first business, she would set up a café. She had found a possible location for a café just off the high street of a local parade of shops in her local area of London.

Objectives

- Understand that customers tend to buy through habit and preference.
- Understand how to analyse these customer buying habits and preferences.
- Understand how businesses can identify market segments.
- Understand how businesses can map their market to set out the key features of the market.
- Understand how businesses use this information to identify and target gaps in the market.

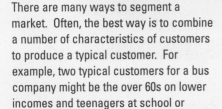

ResultsPlus
Watch Out!

There are many ways to segment a market. Often, the best way is to combine a number of characteristics of customers to produce a typical customer. For example, two typical customers for a bus company might be the over 60s on lower incomes and teenagers at school or college.

Analysing the customer

Before making the decision about whether or not to lease (i.e. rent) the premises for the café, Ruby carefully researched her potential market. She wanted to find out:

- who her potential customers might be;
- what sort of products they would like to buy;
- what sort of prices they would be prepared to pay for their products;
- when they would want to use the services of the café;
- how many times they would use the café;
- whether she could identify any buying habits in her potential customers.

She used a mix of techniques to find her information. She had been attracted to the area because the people who lived there tended to earn high incomes. Because they were affluent (i.e. well off), they had money to spend in cafés. Most people in the locality owned their own homes. She also knew from her own local knowledge of the area that there was a good spread of people of different ages. So there were plenty of young people in their twenties and thirties. There were a good number of young families. But also there were people in their 40s and 50s. They had more income available to spend on 'luxuries' like cafés because they had good jobs. They had paid also off most of their borrowings, including the mortgage on their homes. Then there were the old age pensioners who had plenty of time on their hands and the money to spend in coffee shops.

She also knew that there was a number of small businesses on or near the high street. She made a survey on foot of all the businesses within five minutes walking distance of the potential site for the café. There were estate agents, building societies, insurance brokers, a solicitors and a funeral director, as well as a number of shops. Workers in those businesses could want a cup of coffee or perhaps lunch. So they were potential customers.

Ruby visited a large number of cafes in different areas of London. Some areas were very different from her local area, some were very similar. She would take a photograph of the menu on the outside of the café using her mobile phone. Then at home she would print out a copy. At each café, she would go in and order something off the menu. Then she would take out her notebook and record impressions of the café. What time was it? Who was in the café? What were they eating and drinking? What was the décor and layout like? Were the staff friendly or not and what made them friendly? Did the staff wear uniforms? Of what did the café smell? Did it feel like a successful business or not?

She spent two days, a Wednesday and a Saturday, outside the possible location of her café. She noted down everyone who passed by the premises. For example, she tried to guess their age, whether they were a local worker, retired, or a mum or dad at home looking after the children. Another weekday, she conducted a survey asking people questions like whether they worked in one of the premises in the local area, where they might stop and have a cup of coffee at the moment and where did they get lunch.

Market segments

Ruby knew that there were groups of customers who had similar buying habits. Teenagers between the ages of 14 and 16, for example, tend to buy similar products and buy at the same shops. For some products, though, male teenagers have different buying habits from female teenagers. Businesses can investigate these habits and break their market down into market segments. A **market segment** is a part of a market that contains a group of buyers with similar characteristics.

Ruby used the information she collected to identify three important market segments for her café business.

- The local worker who wanted a good cup of coffee or tea such as can be bought at national coffee chains like Costa. Some of these local workers also wanted a sandwich for lunch. Some would come to the coffee shop but there was also a market for delivery of coffee and sandwiches to their place of work. These local workers wanted a quality product and good service but were not too price sensitive. Being **price sensitive** means that price is very important in your decision about whether or not to buy. The local workers were not too worried about whether the price of a cup of coffee was £1.65 or £1.85 so long as it was good quality.

- Mothers with small children were another important market segment. They wanted a child friendly place to meet with their friends. Quality was important but so too was price. They wanted to feel that they had had good value from what they had bought.

- Then there was the local shopper who would reward themselves with a coffee at the café. This market segment tended to be women of all ages, but particularly those in the 60-75 age range. They wanted friendly service and a feeling that their little treat had not cost too much.

All three sorts of customers would tend to be repeat customers. This means that they would keep coming back to the café for their coffee and sandwiches. She did not expect there to be too many one-off customers. These are customers who buy a product once but are unlikely to buy again.

There are many other ways in which Ruby could have segmented (i.e. split up) her potential market. How a business splits up its market depends very much on the product being sold and who is the customer. For example, businesses could split up their market on:

- age – children, teenagers, 'twenty somethings' and so on;
- gender – male or female;
- income – such as low income, middle income, high income;
- area – for a national company, customers in Scotland, Wales or the South West of England;
- ethnicity – for example, white, Afro-Caribbean, Chinese, Asian;
- religious groups – many religious groups have laws about what they can eat; there is a market for Kosher food for the Jewish community or halal meat for the Muslim community;
- socio-economic group – this refers to whether an individual customer is working class, middle class or upper class.

There is a national classification of this type of grouping called The National

Table 1 – Socio-economic classification

1	Higher managerial and professional occupations
1.1	Large employers and higher managerial occupations
1.2	Higher professional occupations
2	Lower managerial and professional occupations
3	Intermediate occupations
4	Small employers and own account workers
5	Lower supervisory and technical occupations
6	Semi-routine occupations
7	Routine occupations
8	Never worked and long-term unemployed

Market segments in a café - age, gender, income and ethnicity

edexcel ::: key terms

Market segment – part of a market that contains a group of buyers with similar buying habits, such as age or income.

Price sensitive – when the price is very important in the decision about whether or not to buy.

Statistics Socio-economic Classification Analytic Classes (NS-SEC). It classifies people according to the type of occupation they have as shown in Table 1 on the previous page.

Market mapping

Having visited so many cafes, Ruby understood that one café could be very different from another café. She made a list of all the differences. One important difference was price. Then there was the quality of food and drink. Another difference was the atmosphere of the café – whether it was aimed at providing comfortable seating or whether it was a 'greasy spoon' place serving cheap food in a basic setting.

ResultsPlus
Exam Question Report

2 (b) EPP (a cinema) offers a range of products that appeal to different age groups.

(ii) Why does it do this? (8) (June 2006)

How students answered

Some students (36%) scored poorly (ie 0-3) on this question. Some answers simply stated a reason, which almost re-stated the question such as 'to appeal to a range of people'. There was limited explanation of why a business would do this.

Most students (57%) gained good (ie 4-6) marks on this question. These answers would have given reasons, such as appealing to a different range of groups. They explained that people of different age groups have different tastes, for example retired people may go to the cinema in the daytime.

Few students (7%) gained very good (ie 7-8) marks on this question.
Only a few answers gave reasons for extending the product range and offered judgements about why the business did this. These answers considered that increasing the product range would spread the risk and increase sales and market share.

edexcel ⠿ key terms

Market map (or Perceptual map or Positioning map) – a diagram that shows the range of possible positions for two features of a product, such as low to high price and low to high quality.

Gap in the market – occurs when no business is currently serving the needs of customers for a particular product.

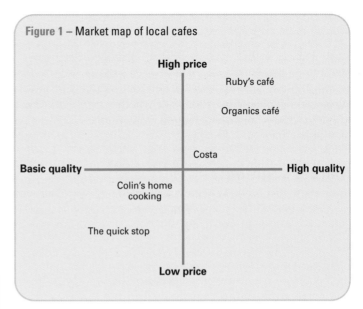

Figure 1 – Market map of local cafes

She then drew a **market map** (also sometimes called a **perceptual map** or a **positioning map**). This is a diagram that shows the range of possible positions for two features of a product. Figure 1 shows the market map drawn by Ruby for local cafes based on her market research. Each name shows an individual café. Ruby has to decide where to put her café. Will her café charge above average prices? In that case, she needs to put her café above the horizontal line. Will her café serve above average quality food and drink? In that case, she needs to put her dot to the right of the vertical line. Given the location of her café, she decides that the best positioning of her café is indeed high price, high quality. So her café will be in the top right hand corner of the diagram.

Ruby could have drawn a number of different market maps each showing different features. One map, for example, could have shown the range of food and drink on offer (from a large range to a small range) and the physical size of the café (from a large floor area to a small floor area).

Market maps show the position of a product or group of products in the market compared to other products. For example, a BMW car is more luxurious than a Nissan Micra. A can of Heinz baked beans is more expensive than a can of value baked beans from a supermarket chain.

Market gaps

There was another café near where Ruby hoped she could open her own café. However, it did not seem very popular. It was a rather old fashioned café serving low quality tea and coffee. Ruby saw that there was a **gap in the market** for her café. A gap in the market occurs when no business is serving the needs of customers for a particular product.

New businesses like Ruby's café can be very successful if they spot a gap in the market and fill that gap. Many new businesses, though, make products that are very similar to other businesses. This too can lead to success if there is a big enough market to be divided up among businesses.

Test yourself

1. A part of a market that contains a group of buyers with similar characteristics is called a market

   A map
   B segment
   C gap
   D resource

   Select one answer.

2. A toy manufacturer sells toys which are linked to a popular television programme aimed at 1-4 year olds. It also sells toys aimed at 5-9 year olds. The two age ranges for the toy manufacturer are examples of market

   A resources
   B maps
   C gaps
   D segments

   Select one answer.

3. Katie Lunn is investigating setting up as an independent newsagent. She has drawn up several market maps to help her in her market research. A market map is a visual means of showing

   Select one answer.

   A where the business is located
   B the conclusions of a market survey
   C where a product is positioned in the market
   D market segments

Over to you

Kendrick King trained as a hair stylist. He became the manager of a hair salon at the age of 23 and then decided that he wanted to set up his own salon. He knew there was a gap in the market in his local area because there were no hairdressers for Afro-Caribbeans. There was a significant population of Afro-Caribbeans where he lived, but the nearest Afro-Caribbean salon was several miles away. Kendrick researched the market carefully visiting a number of Afro-Caribbean salons in other areas to find out what services they offered and what prices they charged. Another part of his market research was to ask all his friends about what they would like to see in a salon.

1. 'There was a gap in the market in his local area.' Explain what is meant by a gap in the market, using Kendrick new salon as an example. (3)

2. What features of the market could Kendrick's have put on a market map to help him position his product? Explain your answer carefully, drawing a market map to help you. (6)

3. Will spotting a gap in the market guarantee that Kendrick's new business will be successful? Justify your answer. (6)

4 Competition

Case Study

Chloe Stirch graduated with a degree in fashion design three years ago. She went on to work at management level for a large department store with much of her work focussed on shoes. Having gained this experience, she feels that now is a good time to launch her own business selling shoes.

Objectives

- Appreciate that initial planning to set up a business will require recognition and investigation into other businesses offering similar products/services (competitors).
- Understand that new businesses will need to find out more about their competitors - their strengths and weaknesses.
- Appreciate that entrepreneurs can spot further opportunities by comparing their business offerings with that of their rivals.

edexcel ::: key terms

Product range – a group of similar products made by a business, like a number of different soap powders.

Analysing the competition

Within the department store, there were a number of different shoe stores (called **concessions**) where each different shoe store rented floor space in the department store and paid the department store a proportion of the money it received in sales. The different shoe stores **competed** with each other for customers. Being able to see their sales figures, Chloe knew that some shoe stores were more successful than others in attracting customers. If she were to set up her own shoe store, she would have to analyse the strengths and weaknesses of her competitors. This might allow her to find a gap in the market.

The shoe stores in her local area fell into three categories. First, there were stores that were part of a national chain. These were stores like Clarks, Ravel, and Barratts. Second, there were local independent stores. These were either owned individually or formed part of a small chain that operated in the local area. Third, there were fashion retailers, department stores and some supermarkets selling clothes which also had an area devoted to selling shoes.

Each shoe outlet had a slightly different **product offering**. This means that individual products were different. So too was the mix (or **product range**) of products for sale. Chloe investigated these and came up with a list of different criteria with which to judge the potential competition.

Product range Shoe stores in the centre of town tended to specialise. There were a large number of stores that only sold women's shoes. She could find only one specialist men's shoes store. Where a shoe store sold both men's and women's shoes the sales area for women's shoes tended to be much larger than for men's shoes. Most shoe stores sold fashion shoes. Independent shoe stores on small parades of shops in the suburbs tended to sell a mix of men's, women's and children's shoes. They tended to sell 'everyday' shoes rather than concentrating on fashion shoes.

Quality Different stores offered different quality products. For example, in more expensive stores, shoes were made of high quality materials such as leather. The quality of manufacture of the shoe was also better. In cheaper stores, many of the shoes were made of plastic or 'imitation leather'. The quality of work could be poor with glue showing on the seam between the uppers of the shoe and the sole, or slight scuff marks on the shoe.

Some stores offer a shopping experience.

Design More expensive shoes tended to have a more elaborate design than cheaper shoes. They are often more comfortable to wear because of design features built into the shoe. So the design helps more expensive shoes to look better and be comfortable.

Selling experience The shopping experience is very important for many customers who buy shoes. At the top end of the market, there are shoe boutiques that are beautifully fitted out. Each shoe is displayed like a piece of art in a museum. There is excellent service. Then there is the stylish bag to take your purchase home. When you are charging £100-£500 for a pair of shoes, customers expect this type of luxury service. At the bottom end of the market, there are the shops that are selling shoes at between £5 and £25. Pairs of shoes are displayed on cheap display racks for customers to try on themselves. The only service is given by the person on the till taking the money.

After-sales service Shoe stores, by law, have to refund monies on shoes that are faulty. But many will also give a refund if the person buying the shoes goes home and decides they do not like them.

Price There are large differences in price between different shoe stores. A pair of ladies' shoes might cost £10 in one store and £500 in another. Chloe noticed that children's shoes that came in a variety of widths as well as size were very expensive in comparison with adult shoes. She also noticed that there seemed to be a narrower range of prices for men's shoes than for women's shoes. Whilst she could find women's shoes priced at £300 in her department store, she couldn't find any men's shoes at that sort of price.

Brand image Chloe was very aware of brand image. A **brand** is a named product which customers see as being different from other products and which has an identity that customers can associate with and recognise. Famous brands include Heinz baked beans, Kellog's cornflakes or a BMW car. **Brand image** is the idea or image that customers have in their minds about the brand. Jimmy Choo and Manolo Blahnik are designer brands. If you buy a pair of shoes from Faith

Watch Out!

Having strong competitors makes it more difficult for a new business to be successful. However, a new business can survive and do well if it can find a different way of doing things, meet the needs of the customers that have been identified as forming the market for the new business and try to match the strength of its competitors. What happens in this situation is that the new competitor takes away sales that would otherwise have gone to another business.

edexcel ⸬ key terms

Brand – a named product which customers see as being different from other products and which they can associate or identify with.

Brand image - the idea/impression/image that customers have in their minds about the brand.

22

and Schuh, the brand image is of a fashionable shoe appealing to teenagers and young people. Clark's has an image of being solid, reliable and safe. It is a place where children as well as mums and dads could find a pair of shoes. The image of a brand is reinforced by advertising. Some shoe brands spent large amounts on advertising and other forms of marketing.

Suppliers Chloe knew that the major shoe chains had very efficient buying teams. These teams had a detailed knowledge of their customers and their needs and travelled the world to find the right product at the right price with the right delivery dates. Most small independent outlets bought their shoes from **wholesalers**. These are businesses that buy from manufacturers worldwide. Then they sell in bulk to individual shoe stores. Some independent outlets, however, bought high fashion branded shoes from a shoe manufacturer. Often they would have the exclusive right to sell these shoes in a local area.

Strengths and weaknesses

From her experience in working at a department store, Chloe knew that the major high street chains of shoe retailers were very competitive. Some seasons, they did not quite get the fashion trends right and lost sales. However, they had had years of experience getting their quality lined up with price, in-store 'experience' and brand image.

Opening a shoe store on the high street that looked like Faith or Clark's would be tough. There was certainly no gap in the market here because their strengths far outweighed their weaknesses.

The local independents had one main strength. They were located near their customers in the suburbs and local shopping parades. However, many of them seemed poorly run to Chloe. Shoes were too often jumbled all together. They often did not seem to be clear whether they were catering to customers who wanted low price, low quality shoes or high price, high quality shoes. The problem for Chloe was that she was not enthusiastic about opening a shoe store trying to cater for everyone from a two year old boy to an 80 year old granny.

So this left her with the idea of opening a shoe store selling exclusive, high quality brands to high-spending, fashion conscious women. There was not an independent shoe store in her local city centre that offered this service. She would need to find the right suppliers that had strong brand images in the minds of her customers. This could be the opportunity that Chloe was seeking. However, she faced one major threat. She would face competition from her own department store. So there would a lot of risk attached to her business venture. She would leave the security of a paid job with promotion prospects at the department store to set up in business on her own.

 Results**Plus**
Build Better Answers

A window cleaning service operating in central Birmingham wants to expand to the outer parts of the city. It has looked at the services offered by its rivals. Which **two** of the following are most likely to show that there is an opportunity for the business to grow?

A   Mike Gibson specialises in cleaning industrial buildings and has a good reputation amongst local businesses.

B   Colin Cain, a rival who works on his own, has a brother who lives in London.

C   Isabela Cioni, the nearest rival, has many friends in the area and is trusted to look after house keys if they are away.

D   Isabela Cioni has recently refused to clean conservatories.

E   Colin Cain is not in the UK for two months every summer.

F   Mike Gibson charges competitive prices.

Answer D and E

Technique guide: There is a number of choices available so first:

Think: What might be the strengths and weaknesses of a window cleaning business? What is the relevance of the 'outer parts of the city' in the question?

Then: Dismiss the choices that are obviously wrong - that would be B ▪

Decide: You are left with A, C, D, E and F. You have narrowed down the options.

Go through these: A, C and F are all strengths of other businesses - quality, services for customers and low prices. ▪

This leaves D and E. They are possible weaknesses. The outer parts of the city is more likely to have houses which may have conservatories - this leaves a gap In the market. If Colin is out of the country that leaves people who will still want their windows cleaning. The business can exploit this. ▲

Over to you

Ellie Morgan is currently the manager of a gym in London. The gym is part of a national chain but things are not going well. The number of clients taking out annual subscriptions has fallen. There are also too few clients coming in and paying a one-off entrance fee for a single session. The equipment and the décor are looking tired and rather shabby. Overall, her branch is losing money. Ellie thinks the gym is likely to be closed within the next 12 months by its owners. This is an opportunity for Ellie to take a different path by opening her own business.

She has a good understanding of the local competition. The market is very crowded. There are national chains of gyms like Esporta that offer good facilities and have a good brand image. They can be a little expensive for customers. However, they seem to have a steady flow of customers.

Then there are the small gyms that are owned by a single person. These are often cheaper for customers although their facilities are usually not as good as the national chains.

Finally, there are gyms that are part of a larger business. There are a couple of hotels in her local area that have a gym for their guests. Local people, though, can also use the gym if they pay. There is also a health spa that offers gym facilities. With both the hotels and the health spa, the gym area is fairly small. However, the equipment is well maintained and some customers like the more intimate atmosphere of the facilities.

With such strong competition, Ellie is not sure she would be able to set up a successful gym on her own. It would need far too much money to set it up. Reading around, though, she found a small business in the Midlands that had had special gym equipment manufactured for primary school children. The machines are much smaller than those for adults. The equipment, together with a trainer, is then hired by primary schools or community centres. Ellie could see a gap in the market in London for this service.

1. Identify **four** different ways in which gyms compete with each other for customers. (4)

2. Analyse why it might be too expensive for Ellie to set up a successful gym aimed at adults. (6)

3. Do you think that Ellie could make a success of a gym for children? Justify your answer. (6)

Test yourself

Read the passage below carefully and then answer questions 1 and 2 that relate to the passage.

Tyler's is a small independent shoe store. It is located in a local high street. A new hypermarket that sells shoes as part of its product offering has just been built at the bottom of the high street. Tyler's has seen its sales fall in recent months and the owner is looking at ways he can compete more effectively.

1. Which **two** of the following methods are most likely to help reduce Tyler's costs in an effort to compete more effectively?

   Select **two** answers.

   A   *Increase its advertising in the local newspaper*
   B   *Provide better service by taking on more staff*
   C   *Increasing the range of its shoes*
   D   *Ordering cheaper shoes from its suppliers*
   E   *Making one member of staff redundant in order to be able to offer lower prices*

2. Which **two** of the following reasons are the most likely explanations for why Tyler's has lost half its sales since the new hypermarket has been built?

   Select **two** answers.

   A   *The hypermarket is a more convenient place for shoppers to buy shoes*
   B   *The level of customer service has got worse at Tyler's*
   C   *The average price of shoes at Tyler's has increased*
   D   *Tyler's has cut its costs by making one of its four staff redundant*
   E   *The hypermarket offers for sale many of the same styles of shoes as Tyler's*

3. A business makes bottled and canned soft drinks. Which of the following in itself is most likely to make it more competitive against its rivals?

   Select **one** answer.

   A   *The employment of two extra workers*
   B   *An increase in profit compared to last year*
   C   *The launch of a new range of drinks*
   D   *A rise in the price of its drinks range*

5 Added value

Case Study

Kamran Younis is in the last year of his degree course in Catering and Food Studies in London. He does not want to get a job working for a company. Instead, he wants to set up his own business. He has always liked chocolate. On his degree course, he has used the time to learn as much as possible about how to make chocolate products. Now he wants to set up in business selling chocolates, based in London.

Objectives

● Understand the meaning of the term 'added value' and explain its importance in business survival and success.

● Appreciate the main sources of added value: convenience and speed, branding, quality, design, and unique selling point.

ResultsPlus
Watch Out!

Added value is the difference between what a business pays its suppliers and what it receives for selling its products. The wages its pays its staff are part of its value added. The workers of a business add value to the output of a business.

edexcel ::: key terms

Added value – the increased worth that a business creates for a product; it is the difference between what a business pays its suppliers and the price that it is able to charge for the product/service.

Added value

Kamran knew there was no point in trying to compete against industry giants like Cadbury, Mars and Nestlé. Products like Yorkie, Aero, Mars Bar and KitKat had massive sales. They were backed by a strong brand image and millions of pounds of advertising and other types of promotion. These chocolate products also had the advantage that they were available widely and in every newsagent and garage shop, not to mention supermarkets. Who would want to sell a different product from an unknown business in their shop?

So Kamran had to find a way of adding value to any product he made. **Added value** is the increased worth that a business creates for a product. For example, a food manufacturer might sell a single chocolate bar for 20p. It pays 5p for the ingredients such as cocoa and sugar, as well as other costs such as the electricity to power machines. It would then add 15p of value for each bar sold. For the business as a whole, it is the difference between the total value of its sales and what it has to pay its suppliers, sometimes referred to as the 'bought in' costs.

Sources of added value

The challenge then for Kamran was to find a product where he could charge more than it would cost him to buy in the raw materials to make the product. He knew that there were many products that were very successful at adding value and that part of their success was in persuading customers to pay the price charged. A pair of Nike trainers, for example, are pretty much the same as a non-branded pair of trainers. They are probably made by the same people in the same factories somewhere, in a country like Indonesia or Vietnam. Somehow, Nike has managed to persuade customers to pay four or five times as much for their trainers as for the non-branded ones. Were they four or five times the quality? Probably not. The real difference was in the fact that the Nike trainers had the famous 'swoosh' on them and that is what added the value.

Kamran decided that the only way to do this was to make high quality, speciality chocolates. These would be sold to restaurants, by mail order and to specialist patisserie (cake) shops. What would then be the main sources of value added in this product? They would be the same as for any business.

High quality chocolates can add value

Quality The quality of his chocolates would be very high. They would therefore appeal to a relatively small group of people who were prepared to pay a high, premium, price for the product.

Design and formula All Kamran's chocolates would be hand-made. They would have a design distinctive from the sort of chocolates found in chocolate selections. They would also have unique formulations. So his chocolates would taste different to the chocolates made by any other manufacturer. Customers would therefore be able to see that the chocolates they were buying and eating were very different. Kamran could also do a design which related to different restaurants and patisseries, so that they would be even more unique. Each restaurant or patisserie would have its 'own chocolates' with its name or logo on them.

Convenience For restaurants and patisseries, buying his chocolates would mean they did not have to produce their own chocolates for sale. A restaurant, for example, might want to have a single chocolate to accompany a coffee. Rather than making the chocolate itself, it might be cheaper and easier to buy in these chocolates. For a patisserie, it might make all its own cakes, but sell a variety of high quality goods made by other manufacturers. It is more convenient and cheaper to buy in these extra goods rather than making them themselves. The addition of the individual design or logo would be an even better selling point.

Speed and quality of service In today's world, customers expect high quality service. A business, for example, expects its suppliers to meet tight delivery schedules. They are prepared to pay a higher price to suppliers that can deliver more quickly than other suppliers or be flexible in responding to customer needs. For example, in London, Kamran would offer next day delivery for orders. Outside of London and for mail order, he would offer 48 hour deliveries.

Branding Over time, Kamran would aim to create a strong brand for his chocolate products. Creating a brand means creating a distinctive product that stands out from those of competitors. The brand image would be one of a high quality, luxury product. Whenever people saw or heard of Kamran's chocolates, these would be the things that they would associate them with.

Unique selling point A **unique selling point**, or USP, is a characteristic of the product that makes it different from other similar products being sold in the

ResultsPlus
Watch Out!

A product may have more than one unique selling point. There could be several ways in which the product is different to other products on the market.

edexcel ::: **key terms**

Unique selling point or USP – a characteristic of a product that makes it different from other similar products being sold in the market such as design, quality or image.

market. The unique selling point could, for example, be the design, quality or level of service associated with a product. For Kamran, the unique selling point had to be the distinct quality of his chocolates. This was the one thing that no other business could copy easily. Very few businesses produced such high quality chocolates as he intended to make. Their chocolate would be different in terms of taste and design from his chocolate.

The importance of value added

Every business, including Kamran's, must add value to survive and be successful. If Kamran pays £12 for

ingredients and sells his chocolates for £10, he makes a loss of £2. If this were to continue, he would be forced to close.

The most successful businesses are the ones that can achieve high levels of value added for the type of product that is being sold. If Kamran can sell his chocolates for £20 when the cost of ingredients is £12, then he has added £8 in value. However, he would be more successful if he could sell his chocolates for £30 when the cost of ingredients is £12. Then he has added £18 in value. The higher the added value, the more likely it is that Kamran's business will survive, grow and be successful in the long term.

ResultsPlus
Build Better Answers

Gemma Mullens lives in Norfolk. Her business is driving people for a night out, taking them to their destination and picking them up. She noticed that people often complain about the service they receive from taxis in the area.

(a) Explain **two** ways in which Gemma could add value to her business. (6)

Basic States up to 2 methods of offering a better service only. (1-2)

Good Identifies up to 2 methods and offers some explanation. The explanation offers up to 3 basic links. A basic link would be 'offering a better quality service (1) by guaranteeing that a car will arrive within 5 minutes of the time it is booked (1). This makes her business convenient for customers who are prepared to pay for this convenience' (1). (3-4)

Excellent Identifies up to 2 methods and offers some explanation. Links are developed clearly and examined in detail. For example, 'offering a better quality service (1) could be by guaranteeing that a car will arrive within 5 minutes of the time it is booked (1). People would have confidence in the business and use its services again (1). The confidence in the quality of the service is valued by customers (1) and they are prepared to pay for this quality (1). As a result, a quality service enables Gemma to add value to her business (1).' (5-6)

Test yourself

1. Jacob Simms is a solo singer who tours the country appearing at concerts and revues. Select **one** answer.

   The added value of his singing business is

   A the total costs of putting on the concerts minus the revenue earned from selling tickets to his concerts
   B what he makes in fees minus his costs such as petrol and hotels
   C the total costs of the concerts at which he appears minus what he has to pay to concert hall owners
   D the wage he pays himself minus what he spends

2. Which **two** of the following might be a source of added value for a farming business? Select **two** answers.

   A Quality of products grown on the farm
   B The wages of the farm workers
   C The profit earned by the farmer
   D Speed of delivery from harvesting to the customer
   E The receipts from sales of farm produce

3. Why is added value important to the survival of a business? Select **one** answer.

   It is important because

   A added value allows a business to target its customers successfully
   B added value always means a better quality of product
   C a business that has negative value added is one that is not likely to be making enough money to pay its costs
   D all businesses have to have a unique selling point

Over to you

Corey Molnar was the manager of a garage. He had worked his way up through the trade, starting at 16 as an apprentice mechanic. Hard work and reliability had led to successive promotions. He had recently inherited a property. He felt that now was the right time to open his own garage business using the money from the sale of the house.

Within a few miles' radius of where he hoped to set up, there were garages for all the major brands of cars such as Ford, Citroen or Toyota. As official franchises of these companies, their mechanics were specially trained to work on these makes of cars. They also only used parts approved by the car manufacturer in services and repairs. Corey knew he had no hope of getting a franchise for a major car company. Instead, he would have to set up as an independent garage. This would keep down the cost of establishing a business anyway.

Competition from other independent garages would be tough. Corey planned to buy an existing garage rather than start the business from scratch. The garage would therefore come with an existing set of customers. However, he planned to expand and make the business more successful. Working as a manager, Corey knew that personal customers valued competitive prices, high quality workmanship and service feedback. The mechanics that did a job would be the ones who would report back to customers on the work done on a car. Corey also wanted to employ a female mechanic who would work on cars delivered by female customers. This could be a big selling point for the business amongst the growing number of female drivers who arranged their own repairs and servicing.

1. Explain **two** ways in which an official franchise garage for a company like Ford or Toyota adds value to the service it provides. (6)

2. Explain **two** unique selling points of Corey Molnar's new business. (6)

3. Do you think that Corey Molnar will make a success of his garage business? Justify your answer. (6)

6 Franchising

Case Study

Toni&Guy is an international company that offers a creative hair styling service. Toni&Guy Hairdressing was founded in London over 40 years ago by Toni and Guy Mascolo. Its styles are varied to reflect customers' different face shapes and lifestyles. In 2008, there were 275 UK salons and another 193 salons internationally. It also had 28 training academies across the world. Gary France worked at Toni&Guy for 15 years as art director. Then he decided that he wanted to set up his own hairdressing business. He decided that, rather than going alone, he would become a franchisee of Toni&Guy.

Objectives

- Understand the principles of franchising as it applies to small business start-ups.
- Appreciate the advantages and disadvantages of using a franchise as a means of starting a new business.
- Assess franchising against other business start-up options.
- Identify a suitable start-up location for a franchise.

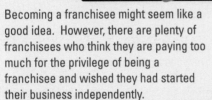

ResultsPlus
Watch Out!

Becoming a franchisee might seem like a good idea. However, there are plenty of franchisees who think they are paying too much for the privilege of being a franchisee and wished they had started their business independently.

edexcel ::: key terms

Franchise – the right given by one business to another to sell goods or services using its name.

Franchisors and franchisees

Toni&Guy is a well known and very successful business. The Toni&Guy brand is associated with high quality and style. Gary knew that the business offered franchises for sale. This means that entrepreneurs can pay a fee to the Toni&Guy organisation to get important benefits. They have the right to use the Toni&Guy name for example. However, they stay as independent businesses. Franchising is one of the ways in which Toni&Guy has expanded. There are many examples of franchise operations, such as Prontaprint, McDonald's, Snappy Snaps, Dominos Pizza and Dyno-Rod.

When Gary investigated buying into a Toni&Guy franchise he found out that the organisation offered part-owned salons that provide hair styling services. Gary could own part of the business and the Toni&Guy organisation would own the remainder. Gary had other options. He could set up his own salon as a sole trader or in partnership with his wife. There was also the option of setting up as a private limited company. However, there were many risks to setting up completely on your own.

Buying into the Toni&Guy franchise meant that Gary had the advantage of running his own business but with the support and success of the Toni&Guy organisation behind him. The investment he had to put into the franchise was quite high but when Gary compared it to the amount he would have to raise to set up entirely on his own he decided that the risk-reward ratio favoured the franchise option. So Gary France, together with his wife, bought 49 per cent of the franchise to a Toni&Guy salon in Kensington in London.

The Toni&Guy franchise developed partly because of the commitment of the business to training staff. Rather than having them set up in competition as rivals, Toni and Guy Mascolo thought it would be far better to allow them to remain part of the business and have the challenge of running their own business whilst spreading the Toni&Guy name.

Many franchises are national or even international companies. They have developed successful products and use their skills and experience to help others to set up in business.

The benefits of a franchise

There are certain advantages to someone like Gary France of using a franchise as the means of starting up a business. In the relationship Gary would be called the **franchisee** and the Toni&Guy organisation the **franchisor**. The advantages include the following.

Training Franchisees usually receive training from the franchisor. Toni&Guy, for example, has academies around the world where it provides basic and advanced training.   This means that the training given by Toni&Guy's is particularly rigorous. Many franchises want to maintain their good name and ensure that franchise operations are successful. Giving the right training is vital.

Equipment Most franchises provide equipment to entrepreneurs as part of the total package. Toni&Guy sells equipment to its franchisees, including hair styling equipment, televisions and its 'salon genius system' computerised till.

Materials to use in the product of a good or service Franchisors typically sell their franchisees some or all of the materials used in production. Toni&Guy franchisees can only use Toni&Guy products in their salons, and not other brands of hair products.

Finding customers Toni&Guy, like other franchises, helps new business owners like Gary find customers through national advertising. It also provides publicity material such as posters. The brand name of 'Toni&Guy', of course, also brings in customers because they are already aware of the business and its reputation. This reduces the risk of failure.

Back up services The franchise package will often come with a range of back up services. Toni&Guy provides advice, loans and insurance cover for example.

A brand name Branding can be crucial to the success of the business. Toni&Guy is known nationally because of its size and its advertising. It has regional managers that check that staff wear uniforms, pictures are correctly used and staff are being properly trained. All this is to make sure that the same high standard is found in every Toni&Guy outlet throughout the world. This helps maintain the quality that customers expect. It provides consistency of customer experience wherever the franchise is located.

Exclusive area Often, new franchise operations are given an exclusive area from which to draw customers. This is true at Toni&Guy. This means that franchises are not in direct competition with each other.

The costs to the franchisee

The franchisor does not provide all its services for nothing. The average amount of money needed to start up a franchise is around £250,000 according to the British Franchise Association. The amount depends on the type of franchise with the more successful ones requiring a greater investment. Franchisors often charge a fixed sum at the start of the franchise agreement to cover the costs of starting up a new branch. Then they usually charge a fee, or royalty, measured as a proportion of the value of everything sold. Sometimes they also charge high prices for the products they sell to the franchisee, making a profit on this. For example, Gary France has a renewable 5 year contract for the Kensington branch of Toni&Guy. He pays a monthly royalty of 10 per cent of sales.

Popular UK franchisees

Watch Out!

The advantages of buying a franchise have to be balanced against the restrictions that exist for the franchisee. A franchise may be a means to run a business but it is not totally independent.

edexcel key terms

Franchisee – a business that agrees to manufacture, distribute or provide a branded product, under licence by a franchisor.

Franchisor – the business that gives franchisees the right to sell its product, in return for a fixed sum of money or a royalty payment.

Advantages for the franchisee

Starting your own business is very risky. There are advantages to buying into a franchise if it can cut down on those risks. There are a number of reasons why risk is reduced.

- The franchisor should select people from those who want to buy a franchise. This tends to eliminate people who are unsuitable for the business.
- The franchisor sets out at the start how much money the franchisee needs to put into the business. Many new businesses fail because the owners badly underestimate the amount of money they will need to survive in business.
- The franchise formula has already been tried out and tested and has been successful. So the franchisee only has to repeat the success of franchises.
- The franchisor provides on-going support and can help the franchisee sort out any problems such as quality control or tax problems.

Disadvantages for the franchisee

Whilst buying into a franchise can help reduce risk and brings advantages from the amount of support given, there are drawbacks.

- The initial investment can be very high and may not be affordable. The payments that have to be made whilst running the business can take away much of the profit from the business. At worst, a business that could have survived making low profits as an independent business is forced into making losses because of the payments it has to make the franchisor.
- The franchisee can not sell the business without the permission of the franchisor. This limits the freedom of a business owner wanting to sell up or close down the business.
- In some franchises, the franchisor can end the franchise arrangement without having to give any reason or pay any compensation. Everything a franchisee has been working for could suddenly disappear.
- Some franchise businesses are more successful than others. Toni&Guy is a highly successful franchise both for its owners and for franchisees. However, with some franchises, too many of the franchisees fail to establish a successful business. Choosing the right franchise is very important for someone wanting to set up in business.

Location

Location is very important for the success of most businesses. Toni&Guy, for example, carefully chooses new locations for its business. The location has to be somewhere busy in the centre of a town where customers can easily get to the hair salon. The same is true for **any** retailing (or shop) location or restaurant location. A fast food chain like McDonald's sites its outlets in the centre of towns. Or they are sited out of town where it is easy to go by car and there are good parking facilities. Franchise operations that work with children tend to use school or church halls so they are convenient for parents to bring their children.

With some franchises, the precise location is less important. If you are operating a domestic cleaning service or a service that provides signs for businesses, the office could be located at home or on an industrial estate. The important thing with these sort of franchise operations is that the franchisee can be contacted by phone, text and email. Services are then taken to the customer. For example, the franchise might be unblocking drains, or replacing a tyre on a car.

ResultsPlus
Build Better Answers

Which **two** of the following would be the **most likely** advantages to a new business becoming a franchisee of Merry Maids, a franchise which provides cleaning services.

A **Working in an area where no other Merry Maids franchise was allowed to set up**
B **Having to arrange your own insurance and loans**
C **Making a loss in the first year**
D **Starting from scratch to find your own customers**
E **Being part of a business that is a household name**
F **Training staff in a new business**

Answer A and E

Technique guide: There is a number of choices available, so first:

Think: What help do new businesses get from joining a franchise?

Then: Dismiss the choices that are obviously wrong - that would be C. ■

Decide: You are left with A B, D, E and F.

Go through these: B, D and F are all potential problems for new businesses that may be prevented if they join a franchise. Training staff can be costly and difficult if the business is new. It can be difficult for new businesses to find customers and arrange loans. Buying into a franchise can reduce the risks associated with these areas. ■

This leaves A and E as the most likely answers. Selling in an area with no competition from another franchise and selling a brand name can help a franchise. Some franchises will have exclusive rights to operate in an area which reduces risk. In addition, buying into a brand that is already successful is easier than having to build the reputation up from scratch. Again, this reduces the risk. ▲

Test yourself

1. Which of the following is a correct statement about franchisees? Select **one** answer.
   - A *Franchisees sell the right to make a product to franchisors*
   - B *Franchisees receive a royalty from franchisors*
   - C *Franchisees receive training and support from franchisors*
   - D *Franchisees sell materials for use in production to franchisors*

2. Which **two** of the following are most likely to be advantages of taking on a franchise. Select **two** answers.
   - A *The franchisor provides a tried and tested product to sell*
   - B *The franchisor pays the franchisee to set up in business*
   - C *The franchisee receives ongoing help and support from the franchisor*
   - D *The franchisor is responsible for paying the taxes of the business*
   - E *Franchisees do not need to have so many business skills as people who set up on their own*

3. Which **two** of the following are most likely to be disadvantages of becoming a franchisee. Select **two** answers.
   - A *Franchises are more likely to fail than businesses which have been set up independently*
   - B *The franchisee has to pay a fee to the franchisor for setting up in business*
   - C *Franchises tend to sell products that are unpopular with customers*
   - D *The franchisee cannot sell the business without the franchisor's permission*
   - E *Franchisees need far more business skills to be successful than people who set up on their own*

Over to you

Merry Maids - domestic cleaning services

Merry Maids is a franchise that provides domestic cleaning services for households. Merry Maids are looking for mature couples or individuals to acquire ownership of a Merry Maids Franchise who have the skills to manage a fast growing business and the cleaning staff who work within it. Merry Maids specialised, two person cleaning concept and accompanying pay incentives attract people who seek part time weekday employment, convenient hours and above average salaries on the quality and quantity of the homes they service. These employees are among Merry Maid's greatest assets. Hence the initial franchise fee charged by Merry Maid also includes an exclusive and unique service worker selection program to make sure you bring the right people into your business.

Also included in the initial franchise fee is the equipment, supplies and exclusive Merry Maids' cleaning products to equip four two person cleaning teams. Each cleaning team, when properly trained and scheduled, can clean two to three homes a day. Merry Maids exclusive Business Management System is yet another important factor that has contributed to the company's position of Market Leader.

Franchise Fee: £9,950 (Plus VAT)
Equipment Package: £5,700 (Plus VAT)
Royalty fee: 7%

ServiceMaster is a successful US franchisor which came to Britain in 1959. Today it has over 900 franchisees in the UK covering 6 different businesses. Two of these are Merry Maids and TruGreen.

Jim and Dot Truepenny are looking to operate a franchise. Jim is 52 and has just been made redundant from his job as a maintenance supervisor, responsible amongst other things for

TruGreen

TruGreen is a franchise opportunity that allows enterprising individuals to enter the profitable and growing lawn care market and provide specialist services on the highest of levels. The franchise benefits from the respected professional standing of its parent company, ServiceMaster limited. It operates with low overheads and attractive margins and is an enjoyable and potentially rewarding business.

TruGreen offers a franchise that means:
- You can work from home, with low overheads, plus great Monday to Friday daytime hours.
- Your franchise will be in the service sector with exceptional growth predictions.
- No cash flow problems and high profit margins.
- 90% repeat customers, in your own territory.

Franchise Fee: £15,000 (Plus VAT)
Equipment Package: £10,500
Royalty fee: 10%

health and safety. Dot works in a garden shop. They are both keen gardeners. Jim was given a redundancy package which included a payment of £22,500.

1. Identify the services being offered by Merry Maids and TruGreen. (2)
2. How much would it cost in total for Jim and Dot to set up (a) a Merry Maids franchise (2) and (b) a TruGreen franchise? (2)
3. Explain **one** advantage and **one** disadvantage to Jim and Dot of setting up in business as a franchisee rather than setting up an independent business. (6)
4. Which of the **two** franchises do you think would most suit Jim and Dot? Justify your answer. (6)

In this topic you have learned about: searching the market carefully and identifying customer needs, the use of market mapping to get the product right and to improve the chances of success, analysing competition and identifying the strengths and weaknesses that a new business has to look at, added value, by which a new business or product establishes itself, the options available to a new business in terms of ownership and how location can affect success.

You should know...

- ☐ Primary research is collected by the business wanting information first hand.
- ☐ Secondary research is looking at other information which other businesses or organisations have collected and published.
- ☐ Quantitative research involves data which can be counted and then analysed to give numerical evidence.
- ☐ Qualitative research involves looking for opinions and reasons for consumers' behaviour to help planning in the business.
- ☐ Data are independent statistics collected by a business.
- ☐ Information is processed data, when two or more items of data are connected to create a new meaning or trend.
- ☐ A survey is what a business uses to find out what already exists.
- ☐ A questionnaire is one method a business uses to collect new data.
- ☐ A market is where buyers and sellers meet to agree to trade.
- ☐ Market mapping is used by an entrepreneur to look at where they see the product or service getting its best chance of success.
- ☐ A market segment is a part of the market with similar buying habits and at which the product or service is aimed. Typical examples are gender, age and employment type.
- ☐ An analysis of competitors is used by a new business to see where it has an advantage over existing businesses, and where problems might lie.
- ☐ Added value is the difference between the price paid by the consumer and the bought in costs - the direct costs of production such as raw materials, component parts etc.

- ☐ Added value could simply be a quantitative value on top of costs to get to a price; or it could be a qualitative value such as 'image' which gets the product noticed.
- ☐ The Unique Selling Point (USP) is what every business wants for its product or service and is often what makes one product sell more quickly than another. It is closely related to added value. The Nike Air Trainer is a good example of both 'added value' (Nike image) and USP (Air cushioning).
- ☐ A franchise is a business opportunity whereby someone can buy the right to sell someone else's idea and product, like a copy of the original.
- ☐ The franchisor sells the franchise. McDonald's is a franchisor. It sells the 'right' to open a new McDonald's.
- ☐ The franchisee buys the franchise, for example, from McDonald's.
- ☐ Location is important for any business; a wrong location could mean a good idea does not stand a chance.
- ☐ Location is especially important for a franchise because the product is already established.
- ☐ Some franchises can be set up anywhere, e.g. a plumbing franchise, but others may need a specific location, e.g. a food franchise needs to be where there are plenty of people.
- ☐ A franchise has advantages such as tested product, national advertising and training.
- ☐ A franchise has disadvantages such as high cost to buy, limited scope to expand and the 'business' is still owned by the franchise.

Support activity

Students could:

- find out and list ten franchises from a range of business activities using the Internet,
- make a list of the different locations and whether they are in or out of town,
- identify the USP or 'added value' of 5 franchises compared with other similar ones, e.g. McDonald's v Burger King,
- take a franchise and identify the target market (customer needs),
- consider how the original business discovered a market.
- conduct a survey of the local high street. How many franchises are there? How many small sole traders? How many 'others'?

Stretch activity

Look at three different franchises in terms of their product or service, business to business (businesses selling to each other) and whether location is critical or they are footloose and can locate anywhere.

Consider the price of the franchise compared with the projected returns and support.

Evaluate in terms of value for money and risk.

Undertake an analysis of the strengths and weaknesses of each.

(a) Bernard lives in the middle of Birmingham. He has been made redundant from his job with a plumbing firm. With the £5,000 he has been given he has decided to buy a franchise. He looked up a list of franchise opportunities on the Internet and settled on Kirsty's Horses. This was a horse sitting service where the business involved looking after horses for owners who had to go away for periods, such as on holiday. Bernard read that the business was very successful so, even though he knew nothing about horses he would give it a try. This will cost him £4,500.

(i) What is a franchise? (1)

(ii) Explain why Bernard might not do well with this franchise. (3)

Think: What is a franchise? Who sells, who buys? What is in this scenario to use in the answer? What are the issues facing Bernard in making this business a success?

Student answer	Examiner comment	Build a better answer
(i) A business where you sell someone else's product like McDonald's.	■ A basic answer including an example.	▲ Use a clear phrase such as 'buying the right to sell a product using someone else's trading name, e.g. Kirsty's Horses.'
(ii) Because he doesn't know much about horses.	■ A basic comment which is correct, but not developed.	▲ Identify one of the problems then link it to others. 'He doesn't know much about horses, so he doesn't know if there is any demand in his local area. The cost of buying into the franchise is using up most of his money so he doesn't seem to have much left to use.' Move the concepts around to get a similar answer. 'He is using up most of his money on buying the franchise so he has not much to play with. He knows the business is successful but he does not have much experience in this business. This could prove to be a problem.'

Practice Exam Questions

Dara Coyle was an excellent cook. She was also keen on growing organic food. Dara often went to garden centres and noticed that many of them had cafés. Although the aroma of the cafés was enticing Dara thought the food was often overpriced and nothing special. She thought she could do better. The idea occurred to her to open up her own business, selling homemade food using home grown products.

Dara decided to do some research and she observed the buying habits of customers at several garden centre cafés. This convinced her there were different groups of buyers and that she could meet the needs of some of them. Dara tried out her menus on some local people who told her they were delighted with the high quality taste of the food, the fact it was local and that they could talk with the 'boss'. Encouraged by this Dara started trading as 'Goodness Nose.' Dara knew that she would face competition from the garden centres and maybe other cafés. However, her research had convinced her that the quality of her products set her apart from the rest, that they would sell and she would make a profit. They might be bigger and cheaper but her products were truly local.

(a) **Two** Unique Selling Points for a product or service could be the

A image of the product
B place to put a price label
C somewhere to advertise
D design of the product
E amount of points the buyer earns on their loyalty card
F strength of the competition (2)

(b) (i) Identify **one** way Dara can add value to her products. (1)
   (ii) Explain how this way will help Dara to add value to her products. (3)

(c) Dara has plans to expand her business through offering it as a franchise if it is a success. In your opinion, would this type of business make a suitable franchise? Justify your answer. (6)

Topic 1.2: Showing enterprise

Topic overview

This topic considers the skills needed to be enterprising. How does creative thinking develop a competitive advantage for a business? What questions do entrepreneurs ask? How can new business ideas come about and how can they be successfully brought to market? Why do calculated risks need to be taken? How will planning, thinking ahead and making connections help a business to be successful?

Case study

Antawan Hayes is a keen cycle rider, but finds that punctures happen too often and always at an inconvenient moment. Antawan is also a keen inventor and entrepreneur. Sometimes, his inventions come from accidental creativity, when he chances upon a discovery. Other times, inventions come from deliberate creativity, when he spends a great deal of time working through a problem. With inventions, lateral thinking is needed. Antawan, like many inventors, finds he has to think of the unusual and unexpected to come up with a solution to a problem.

Last year, Antawan decided to tackle the problem of bicycle tyre punctures. He began to work on the idea of injecting a substance into the tyre, which would automatically find the hole, cover it with a layer of material and repair the puncture. He kept asking himself questions such as 'What?' and 'Why?', 'What if?' He needed to look beyond the obvious.

If he could crack the technical problem, Antawan knew there was a long road ahead of him to get the product to market. An invention protected by a patent was one thing. Successful innovation was another. Planning, thinking ahead, seeing business opportunities and drive and determination were enterprise skills he would need. He also knew that the probability of success was low. There were so many risks that he faced. He thought that he stood a less than 1 in 100 chance of getting an invention stocked in bicycle shops. However, Antawan was not afraid to take risks and was always willing to undertake new ventures.

Having worked on the problem for six months, Antawan could find no satisfactory solution. He weighed up the risks and rewards of continuing to work on the idea and decided that his idea was probably not viable. So he abandoned the work and began searching round for a new idea.

1. Explain whether (a) a bicycle and (b) a bicycle repair at a bicycle repair shop are goods or services.

2. What enterprise skills does an entrepreneur like Antawan need?

3. (a) What is the difference between invention and innovation and (b) why are both important for Antawan's puncture repair idea?

4. Do you think that having a 'less than 1 in 100 chance of getting a successful invention stocked in bicycle shops' means that Antawan should never have spent any time trying to develop his invention? Justify your answer.

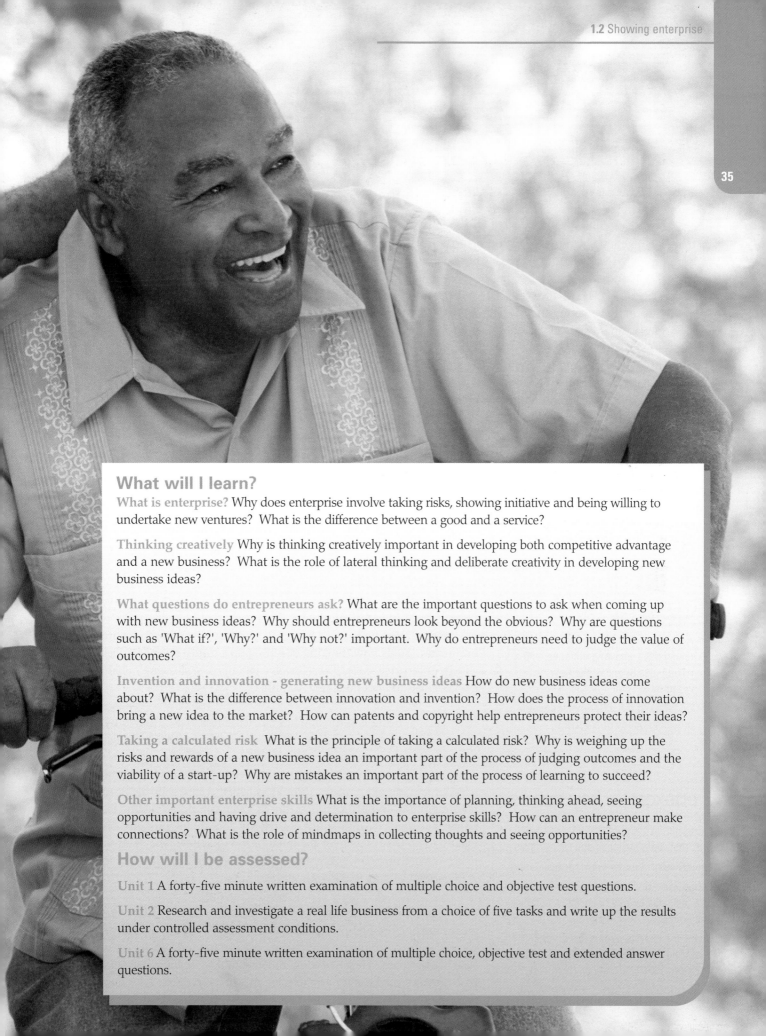

What will I learn?

What is enterprise? Why does enterprise involve taking risks, showing initiative and being willing to undertake new ventures? What is the difference between a good and a service?

Thinking creatively Why is thinking creatively important in developing both competitive advantage and a new business? What is the role of lateral thinking and deliberate creativity in developing new business ideas?

What questions do entrepreneurs ask? What are the important questions to ask when coming up with new business ideas? Why should entrepreneurs look beyond the obvious? Why are questions such as 'What if?', 'Why?' and 'Why not?' important. Why do entrepreneurs need to judge the value of outcomes?

Invention and innovation - generating new business ideas How do new business ideas come about? What is the difference between innovation and invention? How does the process of innovation bring a new idea to the market? How can patents and copyright help entrepreneurs protect their ideas?

Taking a calculated risk What is the principle of taking a calculated risk? Why is weighing up the risks and rewards of a new business idea an important part of the process of judging outcomes and the viability of a start-up? Why are mistakes an important part of the process of learning to succeed?

Other important enterprise skills What is the importance of planning, thinking ahead, seeing opportunities and having drive and determination to enterprise skills? How can an entrepreneur make connections? What is the role of mindmaps in collecting thoughts and seeing opportunities?

How will I be assessed?

Unit 1 A forty-five minute written examination of multiple choice and objective test questions.

Unit 2 Research and investigate a real life business from a choice of five tasks and write up the results under controlled assessment conditions.

Unit 6 A forty-five minute written examination of multiple choice, objective test and extended answer questions.

7 What is enterprise?

Case Study

Dean Fellows is a serial entrepreneur. He is someone who has set up a number of different businesses in his lifetime. He started off working as a cook in a restaurant but soon got bored with that. He quit and spent two years setting up and running a window cleaning business. This did not pay enough, so he set up another business cleaning people's houses. After five years, he sold the business and moved into property development. He brought run down houses, renovated them and then either sold them at a profit or rented them out. The latest property he bought had a fish and chip shop on the ground floor and several flats upstairs. Within six months, the man who rented the fish and chip shop premises handed in notice that he was quitting. Dean could not find anyone to take over the fish and chip shop. So he decided to run it himself using his restaurant experience until he could find a tenant. Twelve months on, Dean is still running the shop. But he has got an idea for a new business: the manufacture of a new type of chip fryer.

Objectives

- Appreciate that enterprise involves taking risks, showing initiative, and a willingness to undertake new ventures.
- Understand the difference between providing goods or a service.

edexcel key terms

Entrepreneur – a person who owns and runs their own business and takes risks.

Enterprises – another word for businesses.

Enterprise – a willingness by an individual or a business to take risks, show initiative and undertake new ventures.

Risk – the chance of damage or loss occurring as a result of making a decision.

Enterprise

Dean Fellows is an **entrepreneur**. This means that he owns and runs his own business and that he is a risk taker. He has already set up three **enterprises** or businesses. He is now thinking of setting up a fourth business. Dean has clearly shown **enterprise** skills. These involve taking risks, showing initiative and having a willingness to undertake new ventures.

Risk taking Being enterprising has an element of **risk**. There are so many things that can go wrong when setting up a business. Dean, for example, found he was not making as much money as he wanted from his window cleaning business. However, worse things could have happened. He might have fallen off a ladder and injured himself. Running a fish and chip shop also could lead to physical injury. In his property business, Dean could find that he loses money rather than gains it. If the price of property goes down, property developers can make a loss. Dean's idea for the manufacture of a new type of chip fryer is also risky. What if no one wants to buy the fryer? What if he finds his idea does not work when he starts making sample products?

Showing initiative Being enterprising involves showing initiative. Initiative means making the first move and making things happen. Dean, for example, showed initiative when he left his job in the factory and set up his own window cleaning business. He is showing initiative in developing a new chip fryer. Dean has shown throughout his working life that he is someone who makes things happen.

A willingness to undertake new ventures A willingness to undertake new ventures is part of being enterprising. Dean has a history of undertaking new ventures. He is always on the look out for new business opportunities. Moving from working in a factory to cleaning houses to running a fish and chip shop all show his ability to take on new challenges. Being willing to take on something new does not mean that you are always successful. For example, Dean's window cleaning business was not successful enough for him to stay with the business. His chip fryer might never get to the stage where it is available for sale to customers. However, Dean is enterprising because he has the courage to quit what is less successful and start something new.

Goods and services

When Dean worked in a factory, he made parts for motor cars. These are classified as **goods**. A good is something tangible and physical. It can be seen and touched. Car parts, kitchen fryers, carpets and lamp posts are all goods.

Most of Dean's working life, though, has been spent providing **services**. Services are products that are intangible. They cannot be touched. Cleaning windows or houses is a service. So too is renting out property or offering take-away meals like fish and chips. When customers buy fish and chips, they buy physical products – the fish, the chips and the wrapping paper for example. But Dean does not make the raw fish, the chips or the wrapping paper, all of which are examples of goods. His fish comes from a supplier. He buys frozen chips from a food manufacturer. The paper comes from a paper manufacturing company. Dean converts these ingredients into a ready meal waiting to be eaten. What Dean provides is a service to his customers.

Take-away outlets like fish and chip shops or a McDonald's are therefore part of the service sector of the economy. So too are restaurants. In fact, most of what is produced today in the UK is services. Over 70 per cent of all the economic activity in the UK is classified as services. This includes education, health care, rubbish collection, shops, banking, public transport and tourism.

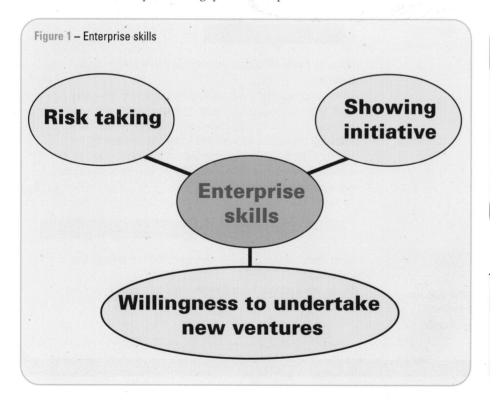

Figure 1 – Enterprise skills

Risk taking

Showing initiative

Enterprise skills

Willingness to undertake new ventures

Results**Plus**
Watch Out!

The word 'enterprise' can be used as another name for a business. But 'enterprise' has another meaning. It describes the willingness of an individual or organisation to take risks, show initiative and undertake new ventures. So enterprise should be a characteristic of all entrepreneurs.

edexcel ::: key terms

Goods – physical, tangible products like a car, a pair of scissors or a television set.

Services – non-physical, intangible products like a taxi journey, a haircut or a television programme.

Test yourself

1. Which **three** of the following are most likely to be examples of being enterprising?

   Select **three** answers.

   A *Being made redundant*
   B *Carrying out an order from your boss*
   C *Taking risks*
   D *Taking the initiative*
   E *Taking your summer holiday at a time convenient for your employer*
   F *Undertaking a new venture*
   G *Being told that your job will change*

2. Which **three** of the following are examples of services?

   Select **three** of the following.

   A *A school desk*
   B *A train carriage*
   C *A tonne of coal*
   D *A train journey*
   E *A knife and fork*
   F *Menu advice in a restaurant*
   G *Education in a state school*

3. Lewis Hunting runs a hairdressers. Which **one** of the following is correct? Select **one** answer.

   A *A haircut is an example of a service*
   B *There are no risks in running a hairdressing business*
   C *A bottle of shampoo is an example of a service*
   D *Lewis Hunting never needs to show initiative in running his business*

 ResultsPlus
Exam Question Report

9. Select the items in the list below that would be considered to be the **four** most important qualities and skills found in an entrepreneur. (4) (May 2008)

   (a) Ability to speak in public
   (b) Determination
   (c) Aggressiveness
   (d) Decisiveness
   (e) Willingness to take risks
   (f) Showing leadership
   (g) Having rich parents
   (h) Being careful to avoid risk

   Answer B, D, E and F

How students answered

 Very few students (1%) scored poorly (ie 0-1) on this question. These answers identified no qualities or just one correct quality, such as determination which is an obvious quality.

Many students (47%) gained good (ie 2-3) marks on this question.
These answers identified two or three qualities. They may have failed to pick up full marks by suggesting that the ability to speak in public or aggressiveness were more important. Although they might be useful in some circumstances, they are not likely to be as important as the four factors stated as correct. A non-aggressive person might also be a successful entrepreneur, for instance.

Most students (52%) gained very good (ie 4) marks on this question.
These answers will have identified the four most important qualities correctly.

Over to you

Charlotte Yelland had always loved horses. As a child, she had done lots of riding and spent as much time as possible at the stables where she kept the horse her parents had bought for her. As an adult, Charlotte had continued to ride even though she could no longer afford to keep a horse of her own.

Her break came when she inherited over half a million pounds. A local stables was up for sale and Charlotte decided to buy it. The stables were not making much money and so it was a risky venture for Charlotte. However, she thought she could turn the business round and establish a successful enterprise.

In her business plan, Charlotte outlined how she would transform the business. Currently, the main source of income was individual horse owners paying to have their horses kept at the stables. Charlotte wanted to open a riding school, offering riding lessons particularly to children. She also wanted to open a shop selling everything a horse rider might need such as

saddles and riding hats. The business would be built up gradually over a five year period to reduce the risk of failure. Charlotte had been advised that very quick expansions often failed. Money to fund the expansion often ran out. Also, the owner could find themselves out of their depth too quickly, without enough time to sort out all the inevitable problems that come with an expanding business. Charlotte, though, hoped that she could build up the business more quickly than the five years proposed in her business plan.

1. Explain why a horse riding hat is an example of a good, but a lesson at a horse riding school is an example of a service. (6)
2. Explain **three** different ways in which Charlotte is showing enterprise. (9)
3. Would it be better if she expanded her business much more quickly than the five years she has put in her business plan? Justify your answer. (6)

8 Thinking creatively

Case Study

Megan Rider has done a lot of jobs in her life. Currently she works in a bag manufacturing business with her husband, Tyler Rider. They wanted to launch their own business and are looking around for a business idea. They were aware that many shops and supermarkets need bags for the goods they sell. They need to think creatively.

Objectives

- Understand that having creative ideas is a key aspect to setting up a new business and developing a competitive advantage.
- Appreciate that sometimes new business ideas come about through lateral thinking.
- Understand the role of deliberate creativity in developing new business ideas.

ResultsPlus
Watch Out!

Gaining a competitive advantage does not mean that a business has to be better at everything compared to other businesses. Being better at one thing is enough for success. For some businesses, simply being the only firm in a local area is enough to give it a competitive advantage. Take a small local corner grocery shop. It can survive if it offers a service to people living around the shop despite the fact that Tesco or Asda offers a much bigger range and has lower prices.

edexcel ::: key terms

Thinking creatively (or creative thinking) – coming up with new and unique ideas.

Competitive advantage – an advantage a business has that enables it to perform better than its rivals in the market and which is both distinctive and defensible.

Deliberate creativity – the intentional creation of new ideas through recognised and accepted techniques.

The importance of creative thinking for entrepreneurs

Many new businesses are not based on creative thinking. Their business idea is a 'Me too' approach – copying someone else's idea. Opening a local corner grocery shop, for example, does not require much creative thinking. There are thousands of such shops around the country. Copying what others do is enough to create a successful business. Franchising is also based on the idea of copying. A franchisee copies the formula of the franchise company to create a successful business.

Thinking creatively means coming up with an idea that is unique and did not exist before. Developing a unique idea can give a new business a **competitive advantage**. Having a competitive advantage means that it is not easy for a competitor to copy an idea, or imitate a product or a method of working. Having a competitive advantage means that a business is better in at least one way than other businesses with which it is in direct competition.

There are many examples of competitive advantage. For example, a business may:

- have a better product than other businesses;
- have a better way of producing what it makes which results in lower costs or better quality;
- give its customers better service;
- be better than its rivals at selling its products to customers;
- come up with an idea or product that is unique;
- use some technology or technique that makes its product or service unique.

Megan and Tyler could create a 'Me too' idea based on the business for which they currently work. However, it will be tough competing with an existing business in the market. So they want to find something new that they can do with their new business. They want to create a competitive advantage.

Deliberate creativity

People think creatively all the time. They come up with new ways of doing things. They respond to new situations. However, most of this type of creative thinking happens accidentally. There is often no method behind how the ideas are generated. The ideas that come out are often not followed up or used in an organised way.

Deliberate creativity uses a range of techniques to stimulate thinking and the production of new ideas. Deliberate creativity involves the use of different methods of thinking. By going through different thought processes, new ideas emerge.

Lateral thinking

To come up with a business idea, Megan and Tyler have gone on a course provided by their local Business Link. This is an organisation paid for by government that promotes business and in particular the setting up of small businesses. On the course, Megan and Tyler are introduced to a number of different techniques in a deliberate attempt to get them to come up with a business idea.

In most situations, people mainly use one way of thinking. Some people tend to be very logical. They think things through step by step. Other people tend to base their decisions on emotions and feelings. Others have a gut reaction as to what to do. They base their decisions on their instincts. Whichever way of thinking is used, the ideas that come up are fairly predictable.

On the Business Link course, Megan and Tyler were introduced to the idea of **lateral thinking**. This is about producing ideas that people would not come up with during their normal day-to-day lives. It is about creating new and unexpected ideas. Sometimes it is described as 'thinking out of the box'.

Megan and Tyler need to engage in lateral thinking if they want to come up with a new business idea that will give them a competitive advantage. There is a variety of techniques that promote lateral thinking including blue skies thinking and Six Thinking Hats.

Blue skies thinking

One commonly used technique in deliberate creative thinking is **blue skies thinking**. There are many ways of blue skies thinking. One way is to start with an idea or an object or a question. Megan and Tyler began their blue skies thinking with a plastic bag they brought home from a supermarket. They put the bag on their kitchen table and then started the next stage of blue skies thinking. They both wrote down anything that came into their minds as they looked at the plastic bag. Figure 1 shows some of the ideas they came up with in 15 minutes.

With blue skies thinking, it is important to bring out as many thoughts as possible. The thoughts or ideas should not be analysed in any way at this stage. No thoughts are 'unimportant' or 'silly' or 'not worth having'. At this stage, the most important thing is to have as many ideas as possible.

The blue skies thinking should stop once participants have run out of ideas. At this stage, the words and ideas that have been written down can be analysed. Which of these ideas is not important? Which could provide an answer to a problem? What needs to be done next to take an idea forward?

Blue skies thinking has helped Megan and Tyler come up with a business idea. Their idea is to produce a range of plastic bin liners for all the different types of dustbins and recycling bins that households now have to use.

Six Thinking Hats

Blue skies thinking involves putting all ideas down on paper. 'Six Thinking Hats' is a technique that helps organise and focus those ideas.

There are many different ways of looking at a problem or issue. 'Six Thinking Hats' takes six different types or styles of thinking. Groups using this technique have to put on the 'hats' one at a time to think about a problem. The six hats are white, red, black, yellow, green and blue. Megan and Tyler used the Six Thinking Hats to explore their business idea about plastic bin liners.

White Hat White hat thinking is about facts. What are the facts about the problem or issue? Megan and Tyler, for example, put down on paper that there are around 25 million households in the UK. Each on average has two bins that are collected at least once every two weeks. If every household used bin liners, that would be a minimum of 1.25 billion bin liners used per year. If just 1 in every 100 households used bin liners, this would be 12.5 million bin liners a year. The

Figure 1

Bag
Plastic
Black
Dustbin
Cheap
On a roll
Refuse
Recycling
Fancydress
Christmas presents
Tip
Lorry
Supermarket
Cupboard
Dirty
Argument
Strong
Ripped
Run out

ResultsPlus
Watch Out!

Lateral thinking can be vital in overcoming problems. However, the solution to a problem is often fairly obvious and does not need any lateral thinking to solve it. If items remain unsold in a shop for over a year, for example, it is almost certainly true that the shop has stock problems. The obvious solution is to get rid of this stock and use the space to sell items that are selling more quickly.

edexcel ⁙ key terms

Lateral thinking – thinking differently to try and find new and unexpected ideas.

Blue skies thinking – a technique of creative thinking where participants are encouraged to think of as many ideas as possible about an issue or a problem.

Mindmaps are sometimes used in blue skies thinking sessions. Participants are asked to think about words as they are put down on a chart. It is a good way of recording the results of blue skies thinking because otherwise ideas are disconnected and it is difficult to see what links the ideas. Mind maps can also be useful to help see the big picture. The centre of the map might be the business but the ideas flowing out of the map can all be separate but linked. A mind map can be helpful in getting an overview of all the different things that businesses have to think about and to see where connections can be made. For example, Max was able to see that being methodical and hard working were strengths of both his planning and his thinking ahead.

Test yourself

Read the following and answer questions 1-3.

Mike Noake is a plumber and he has just set up his own business offering plumbing services mainly to households.

1. Which **one** of the following is most likely to be an example of Mike Noake showing the enterprise skill of 'planning'? Select **one** answer.

   A Answering the phone from a customer who has a leaking pipe
   B Buying a pipe at a plumbers' merchant
   C Calculating how much he needs to save to replace his van in twelve months' time
   D Drawing up the bill for a customer who has had his central heating fixed

2. Which **one** of the following is most likely to be an example of Mike Noake showing the enterprise skill of 'seeing opportunities'? Select **one** answer.

   A Driving to the home of a customer to fix a leaking basin
   B Contacting a local house builder about doing some work for him
   C Changing his mobile phone contract
   D Getting his van repaired after an accident

3. Which **one** of the following is most likely to be an example of Mike Noake showing the enterprise skills of 'drive and determination'? Select **one** answer.

   A Phoning a local house builder five times to see if he has any work for him
   B Filling his van up with petrol every week
   C Arranging insurance for his business once a year
   D Paying his tax on time every month

ResultsPlus
Build better answers

Which **one** of the following is the most likely use for a mind map by an entrepreneur?

A To calculate cash flow in the next six months
B To help staff to find their way round the business' premises
C To plan the costs of a new product.
D To take to a bank to support a loan application
E To provide an overview of key factors that make the business more competitive than its rivals

Answer E

Technique guide: There is a number of choices available so first:

Think: What is a mind map? Why is it used? What is included in a mind map? How might a business use a mind map?

Then: Consider each alternative.

Go through these:

A Is incorrect. An entrepreneur would make use of a cash flow forecast for this. ■

B Is incorrect. This is clearly a wrong distracter that plays on the word 'map'. ■

C Is incorrect. A business would calculate this, perhaps with a budget. ■

D Is unlikely. A business plan would be more suitable for this. ■

E Is the most likely. A mind map can be used to outline the strengths of a business. ▲

Over to you

More and more businesses are closing down. Unemployment is climbing. Sales of new cars are half what they were last year. You would have thought that now is not the time to start a new business. However, Jamie Speke has bucked the trend and launched out on his own.

Jamie has worked for three small engineering firms in his career. In his last job, he was the manager of a small company that made most of its money from maintenance contracts. The company would sign a deal with a customer to give 24 hour 7 day a week service. If a customer's machine broke down, he would go out and repair the machine.

However, Jamie had become frustrated with the company that employed him. The owners did not want to take any risks and were not interested in expanding the business. So he made plans to set up his own business. An opportunity came when a rival business was forced to close. It had been very badly run and Jamie was able to buy its building and machines for a knock down price.

His first priority was to keep the firm's existing customers. Equally important, he went out and found new customers. Some of the more skilled workers were re-employed and new ways of working were introduced which cut costs. By raising sales and cutting costs, Jamie has been able to turn the business around in its first twelve months of operation. It has been hard work for Jamie, but having drive and determination has helped him establish a successful business.

1. Jamie Speke has a number of enterprise skills. Explain **three** of these enterprise skills. (9)
2. Analyse **two** reasons why buying a 'rival business' was a **good** way for Jamie to establish his own successful business. (8)
3. Construct a mindmap to show the issues faced by Jamie in setting up his new business. (6)

Know Zone: Topic 1.2
Showing enterprise

In this topic you have learned about: showing enterprise, such as taking risks and showing initiative, the difference between goods and services, different methods of creative thinking, such as lateral thinking and deliberate creativity, possible questions to be asked by an entrepreneur when starting up a business, the difference between invention, the design of a new product or concept, and innovation, bringing an idea or product successfully to a market, taking calculated risk and the upsides and downsides of new businesses, and the skills that successful entrepreneurs need.

You should know...

☐ Enterprise is an ability to look at something new, in different ways and try to make it happen.

☐ Risk goes with enterprise because a business idea could succeed or fail.

☐ Calculated risk involves using numbers to help decide if the business is likely to succeed. There is more chance if the 'balance' is in favour.

☐ Mistakes could be the result of taking a risk. Mistakes need to be seen as an opportunity to learn, so that the risk in future ventures can be reduced.

☐ Initiative is a willingness to make it happen, not sitting back and waiting for it to happen.

☐ Drive and determination are personal strengths that entrepreneurs need to ensure their idea succeeds.

☐ Creativity is a mind process that involves thinking of what opportunities might exist.

☐ Lateral thinking is a way of looking at something in many different ways, positive and negative. It may give a new look to an idea.

☐ Questioning is a vital part of every stage of a business. Examples include Why? Why not? And What if?

☐ Opportunity is the chance to exploit a gap in the market. It could be created, or it could happen by accident or luck.

☐ Planning is essential. Planning is needed to see if a 'great' idea will actually work in practice.

☐ Mind mapping is a way of writing down thinking. This could be related to the product or could be personal strengths and weaknesses. It is an open-ended analysis.

☐ Connections involve carrying out analysis to see where various parts come together.

☐ Invention is creating and making the new product or service.

☐ Innovation is getting the invention to the right market successfully.

☐ Patents, trademarks and copyright are legal ways to protect the invention from being used by other people without permission. They help create a USP.

Support activity

To help understand the characteristics of entrepreneurs, identify **two** things that you have done successfully. It could be something at school or college or at home. It could be a hobby, a sport or a part-time job.

Make a list of the characteristics you had to show to be successful in your chosen two things. Explain why you needed to show these. For example, did you need to show determination because of setbacks?

What risks did you take? How much luck was involved? How much was hard work?

Now place a tick against all those things that you think are the characteristics that an entrepreneur would need to start up a new business.

In the light of the number of ticks you have highlighted, do you think you have what it takes to be an entrepreneur? Justify your answer.

Stretch activity

Compare **two** products or businesses that have been successful. It could be two products produced by different businesses or two parts of the same business, for example Virgin.

Consider the following questions.

• Were the products new inventions?

• What risks were taken?

• Why did they fail or succeed?

You can use the Internet or past newspapers to help.

Alternatively, search http://www.bized.co.uk for businesses such as Nubrella and MetroNaps. In your opinion will these products become a commercial success? Justify your answer in relation to your knowledge of innovation.

(a) Helen Rodgers has invented a headband that incorporates radio and mp3. It is lightweight and can be customised into a fashion accessory. She realised that once the technology becomes known she would lose the USP of the product and her competitive advantage. In order to recover the costs of the invention and innovation she has taken out a patent.

(i) What is meant by the term 'patent? (1)

(ii) Explain why Helen needs to patent this product. (3)

Think: What is a patent? What does it do? How does it help? What is in this scenario to use in the answer? What is the problem?

Student answer	Examiner comment	Build a better answer
(i) Something you take out on a product to protect it.	■ Just enough to get the mark but does not use clear terminology well. Has left room for doubt in the examiner's mind.	⚠ Use clear phrases such as '… a legal process to stop someone else using the same idea or technology.' Or '… a legal way to protect the idea or method from being used by somebody else as their idea.'
(ii) Because she doesn't want anyone to copy it so she can make a mint.	■ A basic comment which is correct, but not developed.	⚠ Use appropriate terminology in the answer rather than 'street language'. Remember that this is a business course. Identify one of the benefits then link it others. 'She wants to protect her idea from being copied, because she has developed it and paid for the innovation. By protecting it she can get her costs back more quickly as she can charge a high price as she is a monopoly.' Move the concepts around to get a similar answer. 'In order to get her development costs back Helen needs to be able to charge a high price to start with. She could do this if she was the only supplier and, by taking out a patent, she knows nobody can copy it so she will have a USP and be the only supplier.'

Practice Exam Questions

Jason Stait was angry. He was in a restaurant and the service was slow. It wasn't that the waiters weren't working hard, they were. It was the fact that they seemed to waste so much time running back and forward to the kitchen, the till and the phone.

Jason began to think creatively about the problem and came up with the idea of 'i-Waiter'. This would be an electronic device by which waiters could send orders directly to the kitchen. It would have a 'time-received' feature, so the kitchen could prioritise orders. When an order was ready a message would flash on the device to inform the waiter to collect and serve. At the end of the meal the waiter could use the stored order information to produce a bill and accept chip-and-pin payment.

Jason approached his friend Richey Sugg, who was an electronics expert, to help develop the product because he lacked technical knowledge. Jason just knew it would work and he hoped that he could leave his job and set up a successful enterprise. Jason had not run a business before, but he thought that he had the determination and drive to be successful. Jason did some

research and found there was no other product like it. A local restaurant tried it out and agreed Jason was on to a winner. Jason produced a business plan which showed that he would have to spend a lot of money to develop the product.

(a) Which **two** of the following would Jason be **most likely** to do **before** deciding whether to launch the i-Waiter? (2)

A Design a flyer to advertise it
B Get a patent to protect the idea
C Assess the idea using lateral thinking
D Sell shares on the stock exchange to raise money
E Use his savings to buy a restaurant
F Check out the existing competition

(b) Identify and explain **two** questions that Jason, as an entrepreneur, needs to ask about his new business idea. (6)

(c) Do you think that the risks are too great for Jason to go ahead and set up his business? Justify your answer. (6)

Topic 1.3: Putting a business idea into practice

Case study

Claire Critchlow worked in salons and as a mobile beautician. Now she is setting up her own beauty salon in a former doctor's surgery. The salon will offer services and products such as manicures, pedicures, spray tans, sun beds and permanent make-up. Claire's objective to start with is to survive the first year. Then she hopes the business will make a profit and she can open more salons. Facing a challenge and doing something new have always given Claire personal satisfaction. Setting up on her own, as a mobile beautician, gave her a sense of achievement. Now she wants to build something bigger.

Taking on staff will allow Claire to show leadership qualities. She will also need determination and initiative. The project will test her ability to plan, make decisions and take sensible risks. Claire has the backing of a business adviser, Rachael, from a government agency, Business Link. She helped Claire get on courses to develop the skills she would need to set up in business on her own.

Rachael also helped Claire to write a business plan. This is a document that covers all aspects of the business, including finance, marketing and people. In the finance part, Claire had to estimate revenues and costs for the first two years of trading. From this, she was able to forecast the profit for the next two years. She also produced a cash flow forecast. This showed how revenues and costs would affect the amount of cash in the business. The cash flow forecast was vital for survival of the salon. If it ran out of cash, it would be forced to close.

Setting up the business required cash. It was needed for converting the surgery, advertising and buying equipment. Although Claire rented the premises, the landlord wanted a deposit up front. Claire had some savings of her own that she put into the business. Her father gave her some money. She borrowed the rest from the bank.

Success will require hard work and determination from Claire, as well as luck. She has taken advice and prepared a business plan. These will improve her chances of survival in the short term and her success in the long term.

1. Why did Claire want to set up a business?

2. What qualities did she have that might have made her a successful entrepreneur?

3. Why was estimating future revenues, costs, profits and cash flows important for Claire?

4. How did Claire raise the money to start her business?

Topic overview

This topic considers the practicalities of making a business idea happen. What are the objectives in setting up? What are the qualities of a successful entrepreneur? How will estimates of revenues, costs, profits and cash flow fit into the business plan? What sources of finance are available to a start-up business?

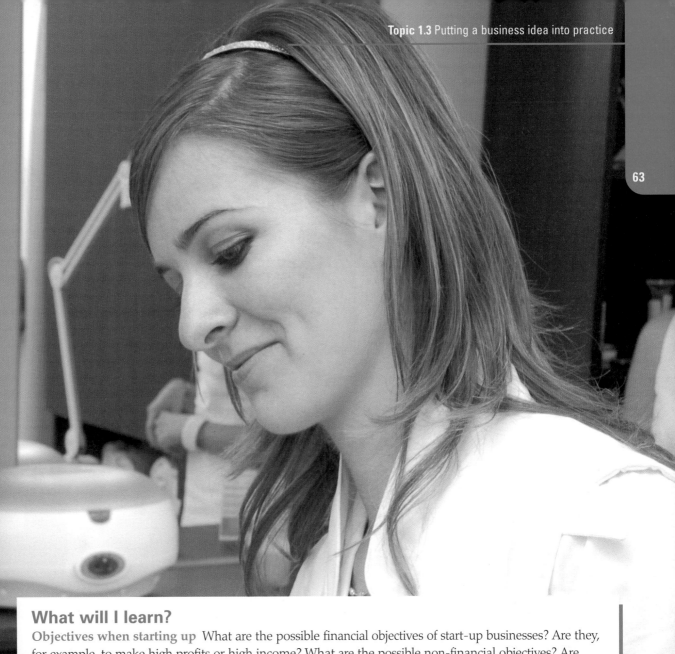

What will I learn?

Objectives when starting up What are the possible financial objectives of start-up businesses? Are they, for example, to make high profits or high income? What are the possible non-financial objectives? Are they, for example, the personal satisfaction that comes from running a business or a desire to help others?

The qualities shown by entrepreneurs What are the qualities of a successful entrepreneur? Examples include determination and taking the initiative, leadership skills and a willingness to take risks.

Estimating revenues, costs and profits How will the number of sales and the prices charged affect revenues? What will be the costs of the business? How will revenues and costs affect profits?

Forecasting cash flows What is cash flow? Why is forecasting cash flow so important for a start-up business? How does a cash flow forecast fit into a business plan?

Obtaining finance What are the main sources of short-term and long-term finance for a business? What is the difference between a loan and an overdraft, or share capital and trade credit?

How will I be assessed?

Unit 1 A forty-five minute written examination of multiple choice and objective test questions.

Unit 2 Research and investigate a real life business from a choice of five tasks and write up the results under controlled assessment conditions.

Unit 6 A forty-five minute written examination of multiple choice, objective test and extended answer questions.

13 Objectives when starting up

Case Study

Jayne and David Shelswell worked for a business that designed websites for the Internet. David worked in sales and Jayne designed the sites. But after a few years, they decided they had had enough. They wanted to set up their own website design business. There was a number of reasons why they wanted to become entrepreneurs, running their own business.

Objectives

- Understand a range of possible financial objectives for an entrepreneur starting up a business, such as profit, income, financial security and wealth.
- Understand a range of possible non-financial objectives of entrepreneurs such as personal satisfaction and challenge.
- Make a distinction between the possible objectives of entrepreneurs starting up a profit-making business and those starting social enterprises.

Financial objectives

Jayne and David wanted to earn more financially. They earned two salaries working for their present employer. But no matter how hard they worked, the amount they could earn was limited. So what were their **financial objectives** in setting up their own business?

Survival Jayne and David were realistic about their new business. They knew that many businesses fail within the first few years. So, to start with, they just wanted to survive. It would take time to build up a base of customers. There would be heavy expenses at the start because they would need to buy computers. They would have to rent premises and buy office equipment. If they could get through this difficult time, they could then achieve the long term financial objectives.

Profit and income Jayne and David knew that in the first year or two, they would have to take a cut in income. But in the long term, they wanted to earn more than their present salaries. So they were motivated by the thought of higher incomes. Their business would pay them a wage. But on top of that, they would also get the profit made by the business.

edexcel key terms

Financial objectives – targets expressed in money terms such as making a profit, earning income or building wealth.

Wealth Jayne and David were also looking forward to their retirement. Their business, if it was successful, could be sold. The price they got for the business would be the value of the wealth they had built up in the business. A successful business would not only mean that they earned more but also that they would become wealthier. That wealth could be used to fund their retirement.

Financial security Owning a business carries risks. What would happen if Jayne and David were to lose important customers? What would happen if the price of new software shot up? What if the business failed? But working for someone else also carries risks. What would happen if Jayne and David were made redundant? Jayne and David felt that owning their own business would give them greater financial security in the long term. Financial security therefore was a long term personal objective for them.

Non-financial objectives

Money was one reason why Jayne and David wanted to set up their own business. But they had other, non-financial, objectives too.

Personal satisfaction Jayne and David looked forward to running their own successful business. They would feel proud and get a great sense of achievement. Building a business would be exciting. They would both get personal satisfaction from their new venture.

ResultsPlus
Watch Out!

Not everyone starting up their own business has the same range of objectives. Some may be very profit driven. Others may be more concerned about their quality of life than earning an extra £1. Treat each case individually and look out for the clues about the motives of the entrepreneurs concerned.

Test yourself

1. Which **three** of the following are the most likely reasons why individuals would want to start in business as a sole trader? Select **three** answers.

A *To increase their earnings*
B *They dislike taking risks*
C *Because they enjoy a challenge*
D *To give them greater control over their future*
E *They prefer to work for someone else*
F *They are afraid of failure*
G *Because they have followed a course in business studies*

2. Which **one** of the following would be a non-financial objective for individuals to start a business? Select **one** answer.

A *To increase income*
B *To get greater work satisfaction*
C *To accumulate wealth*
D *To maximise profit*

Read the passage below carefully and then answer question 3.

Kim Lawton has just set up a restaurant in London. She wants the business to be profitable within six months. After that, she hopes profits will increase sufficiently for her to open a second restaurant within two years. Her personal objective is to own a small chain of restaurants within five years which would make her a wealthy person earning a large amount of money.

3. Which **two** of the following personal objectives does Kim have in opening her restaurant, according to the passage? Select **two** answers.

A *To give customer service*
B *To increase her income*
C *To let someone else make the decisions*
D *To become wealthy*
E *To help others*

66

Challenge Jayne and David both enjoyed a challenge. Creating a successful business from scratch would be their ultimate challenge. Many entrepreneurs like David and Jayne find the challenge of running a business very satisfying.

Independence and control Entrepreneurs like Jayne and David often enjoy the independence that comes with owning a business. They can be their own boss. They don't have to ask anybody else's permission to take time off work. They have more flexibility to organise their lives compared to working for someone else. This gives them more control over how they live their lives.

Helping others Jayne designed posters for charities. Sometimes she would stop and have a chat when she delivered them. She admired how some people were more motivated to work to help others than to earn extra money. A friend of hers, Gemma, had actually helped set up a sports charity working with disadvantaged children on a local estate. Gemma spent most of her spare time unpaid with these children, coaching them in sports.

ResultsPlus
Build Better Answers

Joe Smith has recently set up in business on his own as a plumber. Which **two** of the following would be his financial objectives?

A   Job creation

B   Earning more than in his previous job

C   As a result of a dare

D   Being in control of his hours of work

E   Using profits to fund a pension

F   To keep his family happy

Answer B and E

Technique guide: There is a number of choices available so first:

Think: What is a financial objective? How is it different from a non-financial objective?

Then: Dismiss the choices that are obviously wrong – that would be C. ■

Decide: You are left with A, B, D, E and F. You have narrowed down the options.

Go through these: A, D and F are non-financial objectives - this is why it is important to be clear at the outset what the difference is between financial and non-financial objectives. ■

That leaves you with the correct answers of B and E. They are both financial objectives. Check to make sure your choices are right. ▲

Over to you

When Emma Ratner graduated from university after getting a pharmacy degree, she went to work for a large chain of chemists. Her ambition, though, was always to have her own pharmacy. With financial help from her family and a bank loan, she was able to buy a pharmacy after five years. She was determined to repay the loan as quickly as possible and become financially independent. Within two years, she had increased the profits of the pharmacy 50 per cent by increasing the amount of stock available for sale in the shop. Soon, she was looking to buy a second pharmacy so she could increase her profits further.

Peter Shannon also graduated with a pharmacy degree. Like Emma, he began his working career as a pharmacist at a large high street chain. But it took him ten years to buy his own pharmacy. He enjoyed the contact his own pharmacy gave him with customers. The shop gave him a good profit. But he saw giving a service to the local community as more important than earning extra profit.

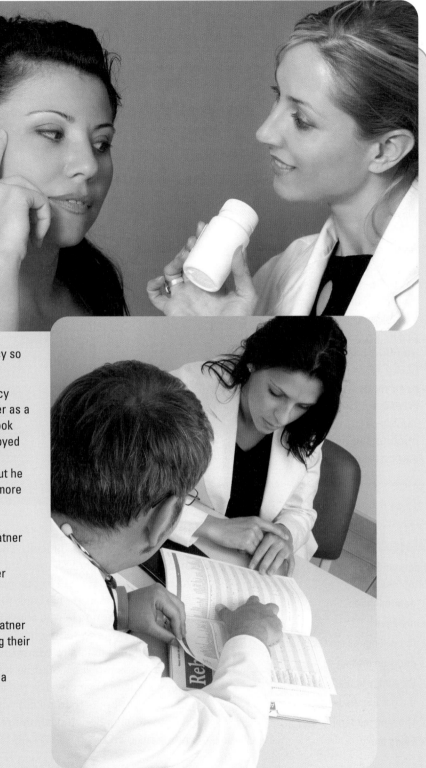

1. Explain **one** financial objective that Emma Ratner might have had in buying her pharmacy. (3)

2. Explain **one** non-financial objective that Peter Shannon might have had when buying his pharmacy. (3)

3. Compare the personal objectives of Emma Ratner with Peter Shannon in setting up and running their own businesses. (6)

4. Do you think that Peter Shannon should buy a second pharmacy like Emma Ratner? Justify your answer. (6)

14 The qualities shown by entrepreneurs

68

Case Study

Rahul Sharma worked for a company which specialised in making plastic goods. He joined the business from university and quickly became a manager. Then he decided to launch his own company. Sharma Plastics manufactures plastic products. For example, a designer plastic table might have been made by the business. What qualities did Rahul have which might make him a successful entrepreneur?

Objectives

Understand the qualities shown by entrepreneurs:

- determination
- initiative
- the willingness to take risks
- decision making
- the ability to plan
- the gift of persuasion
- showing leadership
- being lucky.

Determination

Setting up a business is difficult. There is so much that has to be done before it can start trading. Rahul Sharma, for example, had to find a factory unit from which to operate. He had to buy machinery and hire workers. He also had to get customers and persuade his bank to lend him money. One quality that Rahul had was **determination**. He was able to take control of events. Every step he took brought him closer to setting up his business and then running it successfully. Determination is linked to **commitment**. Rahul could easily have given up when he came across problems. But he was totally committed to setting up and running his own business. For the first two years, he earned less money and worked longer hours than he did when he was working at his former company. But his determination and commitment meant that he stuck to his vision of creating his own business.

Initiative

Entrepreneurs need to be able to take the **initiative**. Initiative means making the first move. They must spot opportunities early and act to take advantage of them. Being **pro-active**, making things happen for their benefit, is important. The opposite of being pro-active is being 're-active', responding to events after they have happened. Being re-active can be dangerous because events can get out of control. Taking the initiative is linked to **being a self-starter**. Entrepreneurs have to work independently. They have to make the first move to start things off. Rahul Sharma had the initiative to set up his own business. He then needed the determination to see his business become successful.

Taking risks

Entrepreneurs have to be **risk takers**. Their business may succeed or it may fail. It is almost always riskier to own your business than to be employed by someone else. Rahul Sharma faced two types of risk when he set up his business. The first was that he borrowed money from the bank at the start. He used his house as security. This meant that, if he failed to keep up the repayments, his bank could take his house and sell it to recover the money. So he risked losing his house if the business failed. The second risk was that the business would underperform. It wouldn't make a big enough profit. The risk was that he would have been better off staying as a worker at his former company.

Entrepreneurs need to be able to plan work and pursuade others

Making decisions

Business owners have to **make decisions**. They are in charge. Being a successful decision maker means being good at making **judgements**. Successful entrepreneurs are often good at taking in information and listening to advice. They have a vision of where they want the business to be in the future. They can then make the right decision for their business. Rahul Sharma had worked as a manager. So he had plenty of practice in making decisions. But he had sometimes been frustrated because his decisions had been overturned by senior managers. Owning his own business meant that he was the boss. Nobody could overturn his decisions because he was at the top of the organisation. But Rahul was also aware that his decisions would now affect the success of his own business. Making the right decisions was even more important than before.

Planning

Running even quite a small business requires some planning. The larger the business, the more important is planning. Entrepreneurs need to be successful planners. This means two things. One is that they know what they want to do with their business. So they have clear objectives. The second is that they have mapped out how they can achieve those objectives. Small businesses are always encouraged by advisers, bankers and government to draw up **business plans**. These are documents giving the objectives of the business and how it will achieve those objectives. Planning is also important on a day-to-day basis. Successful entrepreneurs are often good at organising their own time and planning what their workers will do each day. Running your own business is very time consuming. Time-management is an important skill. Rahul Sharma had experience of planning in his former job. He was able to apply those skills when it came to running his own business.

Persuasion

Entrepreneurs spend time dealing with other people. There are customers and suppliers as well as workers for example. Good entrepreneurs are able to **persuade** others to do what they want them to do. With customers, a successful entrepreneur can persuade them to buy the business's products. With suppliers, it might mean buying at a low price or getting better delivery times. Rahul Sharma was very good at getting the best out of his workers. He could persuade them without difficulty to work overtime if there was a rush order. Where changes were needed, he could persuade them it was for the best to make the changes. The skills of persuasion are closely linked to high levels of people skills – being able to get on with people from a wide range of backgrounds and the ability to create mutual respect.

ResultsPlus
Watch Out!

Do not think that every business owner has to have every skill needed to be a successful entrepreneur. All entrepreneurs have strengths and weaknesses. Good entrepreneurs have enough strengths and few enough weaknesses for them to make a success of running a business. Many of them know their strengths and their weaknesses and are prepared to work at overcoming their weaknesses.

Showing leadership

Entrepreneurs are leaders of their own business. So they should have good **leadership skills**. Having a vision, knowing where the business is heading, being good at planning and having the gift of persuasion are all examples of those skills. Another is **self-confidence**. Successful entrepreneurs have a belief they will succeed. This gives them the confidence to lead their business. Rahul Sharma had considerable self-confidence. He felt that what he had learnt working for his former company had given him the skills to succeed with his own business.

Luck

Businesses need some **luck** to do well. Rahul Sharma created his business in 1996. The economy was doing well and he was able to slowly expand the business. But things might have been very different if the economy had suddenly slowed down. Orders would not have been so easy to get. Or what if had been involved in a serious car accident in 1997 and been unable to work for 12 months? Some entrepreneurs never recover from unlucky events. But others, with the same bad luck, have the skills of **perseverance**. They stick at it when luck does not go their way. They carry on and get through the difficult times. People who give up when the going gets tough are not likely to make good entrepreneurs.

Test yourself

1. In this question, match a quality of an entrepreneur, shown on the left, with an example of that quality, shown on the right. Each quality has only one example. Show each of your five answers by writing out a quality with the example of the quality.

Quality shown by entrepreneurs			Example of quality
Persuasion	1	a	Preparing a production schedule for the next four weeks
Initiative	2	b	Talking a supplier round to giving an extra 2 per cent discount on an order
Luck	3	c	Ordering in 20 per cent more stock in the hope that sales will increase shortly
Risk taking	4	d	Employing a worker who turns out to be much better and more skilled than expected
Planning	5	e	Following the loss of an important customer, deciding to prioritise getting more orders

2. In this question, match a quality of an entrepreneur, shown on the left, with an example of that quality, shown on the right. Each quality has only one example. Show each of your five answers by writing out a quality with the example of the quality.

Quality shown by entrepreneurs			Example of quality
Determination	1	a	Reorganising the layout of the factory
Leadership	2	b	Talking a worker round to doing some overtime
Making decisions	3	c	Having been rejected for a loan by four banks, applying to another bank for the loan
Persuasion	4	d	An ice cream manufacturer has its best sales ever because of the hottest summer on record
Luck	5	e	Having a vision for where the business should be in two years time

Over to you

Michelle Welsman read a newspaper article about a business selling gift wrapping services. She immediately fell in love with the idea and began her research. She found there was no gift wrapping business in her own area and so there would be no competition. But then she began to worry about the money she could lose if her business was not a success. Going out with her new boyfriend also put a limit on the amount of time she could spend on the project. Her family said she should stick with her present job because it brought in a regular salary. Setting up in business was too risky. So she decided to start up the business using what spare time she had. To begin with, she targeted friends and family for orders. But not many orders came in and after six months she abandoned the idea of setting up a business.

Mai Ling Tsui lived in a different part of the country from Michelle. She too read the same newspaper article about a business offering gift wrapping services. Like Michelle, she saw this as a business opportunity. She took some time to research and prepare a business plan which saw her as working part-time in the business at the start, moving to full-time within two years once the business had become established. The plan enabled her to keep control over her costs more easily. Initial costs were kept to a minimum because the business was operated from home. Her only major cost was setting up a website and using the local paper for advertising. After two years, the business was profitable. But Mai Ling decided the profits were not good enough. So she moved on, setting up another business selling bridal gowns.

1. Explain how both Michelle and Mai Ling showed initiative after they had read about the newspaper article. (3)
2. Explain how Mai Ling showed enterprise qualities in setting up her business. (3)
3. Compare Michelle's entrepreneurial qualities with those of Mai Ling's: consider their attitude to risk, their decision making and planning skills and their self-confidence. (8)
4. Do you think that Mai Ling Tsui will make a success of her bridal business? Justify your answer. (6)

 ResultsPlus
Build Better Answers

Diane Frost works for a friend who makes soft furnishings, such a pillows and bedspreads. Her friend is giving up the business, partly for health reasons and partly because profits are falling. Diane knows there is a big contract very soon with a chain of local hotels. Her instinct is to make her friend an offer for the business.

(a) Identify **one** risk Diane has to take. (1)
(b) Explain how she might use entrepreneurial skills to get around this. (3)

Think: What could the risks be? Not enough cash/ the mention that profits are falling/ deal falls through/ no staff. How could she get around it?

■ **Basic** Mentions/ states one risk but offers no explanation. (1)

● **Good** One risk is that there is not enough cash (1). Diane could think ahead (1) to make contact with her bank to arrange finance (1).

▲ **Excellent** One risk is that the profits seem to be falling. (1) Diane could use her initiative to find ways of reversing the falling sales or rising costs (1). She may think about new ways of encouraging sales of soft furnishings or make new designs (1). This could help to reverse the fall in profits (1).

15 Estimating revenues, costs and profits

Case Study

David Lutter was a taxi driver working for a local firm. On Saturdays, he would sometimes be asked to drive a wedding car. Then he had a stroke of luck when he received an inheritance of £30,000. David had been thinking for some time about setting up in business on his own specialising in wedding cars and limousines. This was his opportunity to strike out on his own. Before starting the business, David drew up a business plan. Part of that plan was a section dealing with estimates for his revenues, costs and profits in his first two years of trading.

Objectives

- Understand how businesses forecast sales volumes and selling prices to estimate revenue.

- Understand how to determine fixed and variable costs.

- Understand the difference between price and cost and the concept of profit.

- Explain how profit is the difference between the total revenue generated over a period and the total costs.

- Understand the impact of profits and losses on a business and its owners.

Table 1 – The more jobs done, the higher will be David Lutter's revenues

Number of jobs done	Price per job	Total revenue
10	£100	£1,000
20	£100	£2,000
30	£100	£3,000
40	£100	£4,000

edexcel ::: key terms

Revenues or sales revenue or turnover or sales turnover – the amount of income received from selling goods or services over a period of time.

Sales volume – the number of items or products or services sold by a business over a period of time.

Estimating revenues

David started off by estimating his **revenues**. This is the amount of income his business will earn over a period of time like a week, month or a year. Revenues are sometimes also called **sales revenue**, **turnover**, or **sales turnover**. His revenue will be made up of the money he receives from each job that he does. But to estimate his total revenues, David has to predict:

- how many jobs he will do (called his **sales volume**);
- what will be the average price that he can charge for each job.

Sales volume for David is the number of bookings he makes. People hire limousines for all sorts of occasions. It could be a wedding. It could be to take school leavers to a school prom. He also plans to have a car to take business executives to the airport or to a party. In a typical week, he hopes that he will have 15 bookings. This estimate was based on the casual Saturday work he did for the wedding car hire company. He also asked contacts he knew in four similar local businesses about the amount of work they did in a typical week.

Hiring a wedding car or a limousine is not cheap. For a wedding, for instance, he plans to charge around £400. For taking someone to the airport in a luxury car, he might charge £70. These were the sorts of prices being charged by local competitors. Because each job differs and the price he can charge is different, David has worked out his average price. On average, he predicts he will generate £100 per job.

Now he can work out his estimated weekly revenues. His total revenue is the average selling price multiplied by the sales volume (the quantity sold).

$$\text{Total revenue} = \text{Price} \times \text{Quantity}$$

or

$$TR = P \times Q$$

where TR is total revenue, P is average price and Q is quantity. In this case, Q is the number of jobs that David does.

15 jobs per week, at an average price of £100, is £1,500 per week. The more jobs he does, the higher the revenues as Table 1 shows. It is also true that the higher the average price, the more revenue he makes as Table 2 shows. The two tables tell us that David can increase his revenue either by increasing sales at the same price or increasing his prices if the amount of work he does remains the same.

Estimating costs

There is a number of different costs in running a limousine business. For example, David has to buy the cars he will run. There are petrol, advertising and telephone costs. He also has to pay a wage to himself and his wife who takes the bookings and does the paper work.

Some of these costs stay the same whatever the amount of work that David does. For example, David borrowed the money to buy three cars – a vintage wedding car, a stretch limousine and a Jaguar car. The repayments on the loan are the same whatever the number of bookings that he makes. On his mobile phone contract, he pays a minimum fixed amount per month. He also pays himself and his wife a fixed wage. There is the insurance for the business including his cars. Costs which do not change with output (in this case, the number of jobs that David does) are called **fixed costs**. One very important fact about fixed costs is that they have to be paid even if David has no bookings. Table 3 shows the fixed costs of his business he has to pay each week.

Other costs, called **variable costs**, vary directly with the amount produced. For example, the more miles David drives, the more petrol he uses. So petrol is a variable cost for David. For some bookings, passengers are given a 'free' bottle of champagne. The bottle of champagne is a variable cost to the business. Table 4 shows the estimated weekly variable costs, assuming that he does 15 jobs per week. The more jobs he does, the higher the variable costs. Variable costs would be zero if he did no jobs at all.

Fixed costs plus variable costs add up to **total costs**. This can be shown in the formula

$$TC = FC + VC$$

where TC is total cost, FC is fixed cost and VC is variable cost.

Having researched all his costs, David has estimated that his total cost will add up to £1,400 per week for 15 jobs.

Table 2 – The higher the price per job, the higher will be David Lutter's revenues

Number of jobs done	Price per job	Total revenue
10	£100	£1,000
10	£200	£2,000
10	£300	£3,000
10	£400	£4,000

Watch Out!

Forecasts and estimates may be very accurate. But in the case of a small start-up business, forecasting sales and costs over the first twelve months of operation is very difficult. Many new businesses fail because they overestimate revenues and underestimate costs.

Watch Out!

Total revenues and total costs are over a period of time. Always make sure you understand whether it is, for example, a day, a week, a month, a quarter (three months) or a year.

edexcel key terms

Fixed costs – costs which do not vary with the output produced such as rent, business rates, advertising costs, administration costs and salaries.

Total costs – all the costs of a business; it is equal to fixed costs plus variable costs.

Variable costs – costs which change directly with the number of products made by a business such as the cost of buying raw materials.

Table 3 – Fixed costs per week for David Lutter

	£
Repayments on loan	£300
Wages of permanent workers	£710
Web site and phones	£60
Advertising	£40
Insurance	£90
Total fixed costs	**£1,200**

Table 4 – Variable costs per week for David Lutter for 15 jobs.

	£
Fuel	£110
Wages of casual staff	£30
Champagne and other refreshments	£40
Car valeting (cleaning cars)	£20
Total variable costs	**£200**

74

Price, cost and profit

When David earns £100 for a job, what happens to the money? The £100 has to be used to cover his costs. He has to pay his bills and the wages to staff. There is tax to pay to the government as well. If his costs are £90, then he has made a **profit** on the job. If his costs come to more than £100, then he makes a **loss**. So the difference between the price paid and the cost is either profit or loss.

Total revenue, total cost and profit

On a weekly basis, his profit is the difference between total revenue and total costs for the week.

Profit/Loss = Total revenue − Total cost

David has estimated that his weekly total revenue will be £1,500. He has also estimated that his weekly total costs will be £1,400. So his estimated weekly profit is £100 (£1,500 - £1,400).

His estimates could turn out to be wrong. Many start-up businesses overestimate their revenues and underestimate their costs. If

- David only has total revenues of £1,000 per week and
- his total weekly costs are £1,500 then
- he will make a loss of £500 (£1,000 - £1,500).

The impact of profits and losses

David estimated that his business would show a small profit in its first year. His 'guesstimate' was £100 per week. This would amount to £5,200 (52 x £100) per year. But he also knew he could easily have been too optimistic. His guesses and estimates might be wrong.

- What if the price of petrol went up?
- What if the cars cost more to buy than he thought?
- What if the cost of insurance was higher?
- What if he didn't get the number of jobs he estimated?
- What if it took much longer for him to build up his customer base?
- What if competition was so fierce that he was forced to offer much lower prices?
- What if the interest rate on his bank loans went up?
- What if the economy took a downturn and some people could no longer afford the luxury of hiring a limousine?

The £30,000 he inherited was a cushion in case things went badly wrong and he made a big loss in his first year. He could survive. But if he carried on making losses, eventually he would be forced to close the business. Losses are a sign that the business needs to make changes or close.

Businesses that make profit can survive. Profit is also a sign of whether a business should grow in size. Could the business make even bigger profits by expanding? If nothing else, large profits give a business the money to pay for new investment. Large profits also provide the incentive to make the business successful.

ResultsPlus
Watch Out!

Price and cost are sometimes used to mean the same thing but sometimes they refer to two completely different things. The price of a product is the amount paid by the customer who buys the product. So the cost to the customer of buying the product is the same here as price. But the cost to the producer is different. Cost in this sense refers to the cost of production. Usually in Business Studies, the word 'cost' means the cost of production. Price means the price paid for a product.

ResultsPlus
Watch Out!

Making a profit is not necessarily a sign of success. What if a business makes a profit of £10 a year? If a business does not make enough profit, its owners may close the business. Equally, making a loss isn't necessarily bad. Start-up businesses often make losses when they first begin trading. It is large losses over a period of time that force businesses to close.

edexcel ::: key terms

Profit – occurs when the revenues of a business are greater than its costs over a period of time.

Loss – occurs when the revenues of a business are less than its costs over a period of time.

ResultsPlus
Build Better Answers

A construction business builds flats. It buys raw materials from local suppliers. Joey Simms is the construction manager. He is paid a salary each year, but does not earn bonuses or overtime. He works in an office in Norwich, which the business rents each month. Which **one** of the following is the best example of a variable cost?

A The yearly salary of a construction manager
B The rent paid for the offices
C Insurance for the business
D Cement used in the construction of the buildings

Answer C

Think: What costs change as output changes? What costs stay the same as output changes?

Then: Go through these. A, B and C are all costs that do not change as output changes. They are fixed costs. A construction manager will be paid a fixed salary a year. Rent for offices is a fixed payment. So is the insurance payment.

This leaves you with the correct answer of C. Variable costs increase as output increases. As more flats are built, the cost of materials like cement used in the production of flats will increase.

Test yourself

1. Which **three** of the following are examples of variable costs? Select **three** answers.

   A Rent on a factory unit
   B The cost of clothes bought by a high street fashion boutique
   C Advertising in a local newspaper
   D The salary of the managing director of a company
   E Coca-Cola drinks in a fast food restaurant
   F Diesel fuel used by a taxi driver
   G The interest on a loan

2. A paint ball business charges customers £10 for each paint ball session. Last year customers paid for 5,000 sessions. This year, it increased its prices to £11 but the number of sessions sold fell to 4,000. What effect will this have had on revenues? Select **one** answer.

   A increase by 10 per cent
   B fall by £10,000
   C change from £50,000 to £44,000
   D increase by £1,000

3. A maker of electric guitars has fixed costs of £2,000 per month. Last month, it manufactured 50 guitars items. Its variable cost was £70 per guitar. This month, it has produced 60 guitars and the variable cost per guitar has stayed the same. What effect will this have on its total costs? Select **one** answer. Its total cost will increase:

   A by 20 per cent
   B by £700
   C from £3,500 to £4,200
   D by £70

Over to you

Pets Havens is a business which is now two years old. Set up by Kevin and Emma, it provides a mobile pet-grooming service. They decided there was a gap in the market in their local area of Bournemouth and hope to expand the business to cover other services such as providing kennels for overnight accommodation for pets.

To start the business, they took out a loan for £20,000 repayable over five years. Most of this was used to pay for two vans. A small van transports equipment to allow grooming in the client's home. A large van acts as mobile premises and 'doggie makeovers' are given in the van itself. Around £5,000 was used to buy equipment for the business and set up a website. Kevin and Emma are paying back the loan at a rate of £400 per month.

They have a variety of other costs which stay the same however much work they complete. For example, they pay an accountant to sort out their finances. They have to pay insurance on their vans and for their business. They also advertise in *Yellow Pages*. These costs add up to £5,200 a year.

Each visit they make to a client costs money too. There are petrol costs as well as the cost of shampoos and other grooming materials. These costs work out at £5 per session.

The average price they charge clients is £20 per session. Kevin and Emma complete around ten sessions a day, which, by the time you take holidays into account, is 2,000 sessions a year.

1. Make a list of Kevin and Emma's (a) fixed costs and (b) variable costs in running their business that are mentioned in the passage. (4)

2. (a) How many pet grooming sessions do they sell each year? (b) What is the average price paid by customers for each pet grooming session? (c) What is Kevin and Emma's total sales revenue for the year? (3)

3. Kevin and Emma have worked out that their total fixed costs are £10,000 per year. Explain how they calculated this. (3)

4. (a) What is their variable cost per pet grooming session? (b) What are their total variable costs per year? (2)

5. Calculate the value of their total costs. (3)

6. How much profit do they make over a year giving 2,000 pet grooming sessions? (3)

7. Would they have made a profit if they had only completed 400 sessions in a year? Explain your answer. (6)

8. What might be the advantages and disadvantages for them of expanding their business to offer kennels for overnight accommodation of pets? (9)

16 Forecasting cash flows

Case Study

Holly Buckley worked at a local arts centre. She had learnt flower arranging skills as part of her college course. Holly decided to set up a business providing flower arrangements called Floral Events. She would run this from a shop in the town centre. Weddings were likely to be a big market, but Holly also thought that flower arrangements would be needed for sports events and festivals.

Objectives

- Understand the role and importance of cash flow to a business.
- Estimate cash flows.
- Understand the difference between a cash flow forecast (an estimate) and a cash flow statement (what has actually happened).
- Explain how cash flow problems arise and how they can be minimised.
- Explain how cash flow problems can affect a business.
- Appreciate how careful planning can minimise risk.

Results Plus
Watch Out!

Cash flow is NOT the same as profit. Profit is sales revenue (price x quantity sold) minus costs. Cash flow is all inflows of cash minus all outflows of cash.

edexcel key terms

Cash – notes, coins and money in the bank.
Cash flow – the flow of cash into and out of a business.
Inflow – the cash flowing into a business, its **receipts**.
Outflow – the cash flowing out of a business, its **payments**.

Cash

Holly knew that **cash** is vital for the success of a business. Cash is not just notes and coins. It is also money in the bank. Holly needed cash to start up her business. For example, she had to pay for shelves and equipment in her shop. Once she opened the shop, she had regular bills to pay. There was rent, telephone and electricity bills and wages. She also had to buy the flowers to sell. Holly paid some bills with notes and coins. Most bills, though, she paid directly out of her bank account. Cash came into the business too. Customers paid her cash for the flowers she sold. Every day, Holly would go to the bank to deposit her takings.

What is cash flow?

Cash flow is the flow of money into and out of a business.

Inflows Inflows are the cash coming into the business
- Holly put some of her own money into the business.
- She took out a small loan from the bank.
- The business received cash from its sales.

Inflows are the **receipts** of the business - the money it receives. Figure 1 shows these **inflows** from Holly's business in its first six months.

Outflows Outflows are the cash going out of the business. Holly had a number of outflows.
- Wages.
- Equipment.
- Telephone, gas and electricity and other bills, and rent for the premises.
- Flowers and display stands from suppliers.
- Interest on the loan.
- Advertising in local papers.

Outflows are the **payments** of the business to others. Figure 2 shows these **outflows** from Holly's business in its first six months.

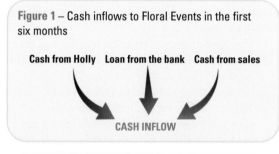

Figure 1 – Cash inflows to Floral Events in the first six months

Figure 2 – Cash outflows from Floral Events in the first six months

Cash flows can be shown in a table. Table 1 shows the cash inflows and outflows from Holly's business in its first month. The **net cash flow** is inflows minus outflows. It is the difference between receipts and payments. £2,400 came into the business in the first month. £2,200 left the business. So the net cash flow was £200.

The importance of cash

Holly's business cannot survive without cash. Imagine what would happen if Holly didn't have the cash to pay her bills. Her creditors, anyone to whom she owes money, would take her to court to recover their money. But by this time her business could have failed. Her workers could have left because they were not being paid. Her flower suppliers could have stopped deliveries because they weren't getting paid. The business would become **insolvent**.

A business needs enough cash to survive on a day-to-day basis. If Holly runs out of cash, she might have enough cash of her own to put into the business. Or perhaps Holly could persuade her bank to give her a loan. Completely running out of cash almost certainly means the business will fail.

Cash flow forecasts

Cash is vital for the success of a business. So Holly must plan ahead to make sure she will always have enough cash in the business to survive. She does this by producing a **cash flow forecast**. A cash flow forecast is a prediction of how cash will flow into and out of a business in future. Businesses use cash flow forecasts:
- to see how well they should be performing in the near future: cash flow forecasts are part of a business plan;
- to see if action needs to be taken to avoid a cash crisis;
- to take to the bank if the business needs a loan to cover a shortage of cash.

Table 2 shows the cash flow forecast for Floral Events during the first 6 months of the business. Look down the column for January.
- Total receipts, all the cash coming into Floral Events, was £2,400.
- Total payments, all the cash going out of the business, was £2,200.
- Net cash flow was £200. This is total receipts minus total payments: £2,400 - £2,200 = £200.
- The **opening balance** is the cash balance at the start of the month. In January when the business starts, it is zero.
- The net cash flow is added to the opening balance to give the **closing balance**. In January the opening balance is 0 and adding net cash flow of £200 gives a closing balance of £0 + £200 = £200. The closing balance becomes the opening balance for next month. The closing balance shows the **cumulative cash flow** of the business.

Table 1 – Inflows and outflows

	Jan (£)
Receipts/inflows	
Sales	600
Cash from Holly	1,000
Loan	800
Total receipts	**2,400**
Payments/outflows	
Equipment	200
Wages	200
Bills	400
Interest	100
Materials	1,200
Advertising	100
Total payments	**2,200**
Net cash flow	**200**

ResultsPlus
Watch Out!

More money in than out is a SURPLUS (not profit). Less money in than out is a SHORTFALL (not loss). Do not refer to them as profit and loss.

edexcel ::: key terms

Net cash flow – the receipts of a business minus its payments.

Insolvency – when a business can no longer pay its debts.

Cash flow forecast – a prediction of how cash will flow through a business in a period of time in future.

Opening balance – the amount of money in a business at the start of a month.

Closing balance – the amount of money in a business at the end of a month.

Cumulative cash flow – the sum of cash that flows into a business over time.

Table 2 – Cash flow forecast for Floral Events during the first 6 months of the business

(£)	January	February	March	April	May	June
Receipts	2,400	2,400	3,000	3,400	4,500	5,000
Payments	2,200	2,500	3,400	4,000	4,200	4,200
Net cash flow	200	-100	-400	-600	300	800
Opening balance	0	200	100	-300	-900	-600
Closing balance	**200**	**100**	**-300**	**-900**	**-600**	**200**

Cash flow problems

Look at Table 2. Does Floral Events have a cash flow problem?

- Look across the table, along the line for net cash flow. It shows that more cash leaves the business between February and April than comes in. This could be a problem if the business runs out of cash.
- Look across the table, along the line for the closing balance. This shows how much cash is left in the business at the end of the month. In March, this is negative (-£300). This shows that during the month, the business has run out of cash. At this point, Holly's business will almost certainly fail.

So Holly's cash flow forecast shows her that her business probably won't survive the first few months of trading. She will have to take action to avoid this by:

- increasing sales revenues;
- reducing costs;
- putting more of her own money into the business or getting a bigger bank loan.

Table 2 also shows that her problems are temporary. In May and June, monthly cash flow becomes positive. By the end of June, the closing balance has turned positive. This is goods news. But to survive to the end of June, Holly first has to sort out the cash flow crisis in March.

What affects cash flow?

Cash flows into and out of a business. There are different things which affect how much cash comes in and how much goes out.

Sales can change At Floral Events, summer is busier than winter because there are more weddings and more orders for flowers. Mother's day gives a huge boost to cash coming into the business as people buy flowers. For many local clothes boutiques near to Floral Events, half of all sales are between September and Christmas. Events like sales can help boost cash into the business.

Costs can change Table 1 shows the costs for Floral Events. The price of flowers from growers has been going up over time. Gas and electricity prices can change. Wages go up each year. Any increase in costs will lead to higher flows of cash out of the business. Every business needs to keep its costs under control to avoid cash flow problems.

Credit terms can change Typically, a business does not have to pay for goods and services it receives until after they have been delivered. This is called **trade credit**. It is a form of loan given by a business to a customer. At Floral Events, most bills have to be paid within a month. But like many small businesses, if Holly doesn't have the cash to pay the bill, she delays the payment. So she might pay a bill after two months or three months. This improves her cash flow

temporarily because cash is not flowing out of the business as quickly. If she doesn't eventually pay her bills, her suppliers will stop supplying her with flowers and electricity.

Floral Events is lucky because most of its sales are for cash on delivery. In her shop, customers pay cash. For weddings, she insists on payment when the flowers are delivered. But for sports events and festivals, she has to give her customers trade credit. Where possible, she only gives two weeks to pay rather than one month. This makes the cash come in more quickly and so improves her cash flow.

Stock levels can change Stocks are materials held by a business. For example, Floral Events holds stocks of fresh and dried flowers, waiting for sale. A car manufacturer would hold stocks of steel, paint, car engines and finished cars. Buying in stock means an outflow of cash. Selling the stock means that cash comes into the business. So stock levels affect cash flow. Increasing stocks without increasing

edexcel key terms

Trade credit – where a supplier gives a customer a period of time to pay a bill (or invoice) for goods or services once they have been delivered.

Stocks – materials that a business holds. Some could be materials waiting to be used in the production process and some could be finished stock waiting to be delivered to customers.

ResultsPlus
Build Better Answers

(a) Identify **one** factor that can affect the cash flow of a business. (1)

(b) Explain how this factor can lead to a cash flow problem. (3)

Think: What factors affect cash flow? What is a cash flow problem? How do changes in these factors affect cash flow?

■ **Basic** Mentions one factor but offers no explanation or an incorrect explanation. (1)

● **Good** Identifies one factor and offers some explanation that shows how it might lead to a cash flow problem. The explanation offers up to 2 basic links to show the effect on cash flow. A basic link would be 'a rise in costs will increase outgoings.' (2-3)

▲ **Excellent** Identifies one factor and offers an explanation that shows how it might lead to a cash flow problem. The explanation offers up to 3 basic links to show the effect on cash flow. For example, 'a rise in costs will increase outgoings, if inflows remain the same, the business will have less cash available.' (4)

sales will lead to a worsening of the cash flow position. If Floral Events buys lots of dried flowers but doesn't sell them, it will have more stocks of dried flowers in its shop. But its cash flow situation will worsen because the dried flowers will have to be paid for and so cash will flow out.

The importance of planning

How can a business avoid cash flow problems? Careful planning will help. Many strategies are possible, but a good rule of thumb would be 'GET IT':

- **G**et the help and support of the bank and investors.
- **E**nsure market research is thorough.
- **T**houghtful cash flow planning may avoid problems.
- **I**nvestigate where you can get help with spreading payments more evenly.
- **T**rack the actual cash flow against the forecast before it becomes a problem.

Test yourself

1. A small bakery has just launched a new range of cakes. Which of the following is not a cash inflow for the small bakery business? Select **one** answer.

   A Capital from the owner to help launch the range
   B Buying ingredients for the cakes
   C A loan to help launch the range
   D Sales from the new range of cakes

2. A business has a produced a cash flow forecast for January.
   Total receipts of the business are £17,000.
   Total payments are £15,000.
   The opening balance is £10,000.
   What will be the net cash flow at the end of January? Select **one** answer.

   A £10,000
   B £12,000
   C £2,000
   D £32,000

3. The following table shows the cash flow forecast for business for three months of the year. Fill in the blanks.

(£)	June	July	August
Total receipts	60,000		78,000
Payments			
Materials		30,000	42,000
Other costs	60,000	75,000	85,000
Total payments	80,000	105,000	127,000
Net cash flow	-20,000	-35,000	
Opening balance	30,000		-25,000
Closing balance	10,000	-25,000	-74,000

Over to you

Aziz Duah decided to set up a business selling printed t-shirts. He researched the market and found that there was no-one in the area offering this service. He thought that selling to businesses or to up and coming bands for their fans would be successful.

Aziz would offer to design and print the t-shirts with their own designs. He would begin trading in September. His sales forecast included the following information.

Receipts
- September £14,000, October £15,000, November £18,500 and December £19,500

Payments
- Machinery and office equipment are £9,000 in September.
- Wages are £5,000 in September and October and £10,000 in November and December.
- Heating and lighting are £1,000 a quarter. The first payment is October.
- Other costs are £2,200 a month.
- Materials are £2,000 a month in September, October and November. In December Aziz plans to arrange a 30 day payment period for materials.
- Insurance is £3,500 for the year, payable in October.
- There is no opening cash balance.

(£)	Sept	Oct	Nov	Dec
Total receipts	14,000	15,000	8,500	19,500
Payments				
Machinery/equipment	9,000	0	0	0
Wages	5,000	5,000	10,000	10,000
Heating & lighting	0	1,000	0	0
Other costs	2,200	2,200	2,200	2,200
Materials	2,000	2,000	2,000	0
Insurance	0	3,500	0	0
Total payments	18,200		14,200	12,200
Net cash flow		1,300	5,700	
Opening balance	0	-4,200	-2,900	1,400
Closing balance	-4,200	-2,900		8,700

1. Calculate the missing figures in the table. (4)
2. Explain why the business has a cash flow problem in September but not December. (6)
3. Aziz is thinking of taking out a long-term bank loan to improve cash flow. Do you think he should do this? Justify your answer. (6)

17 The business plan

Case Study

Chloe and Samir met at primary school and have been friends ever since. Chloe has been working for a construction company for the past five years, whilst Samir has done a variety of office jobs, including some accounting and designing. Chloe would like to set up her own business, which would specialise in shop fitting. This sort of business designs the inside of shops and fits everything from shelves and counters to lighting and tills. Samir has agreed to give up his current job to join her. Finance is going to be tight and they have talked through their ideas with several banks to find out if they could borrow money. All the banks have said that any loan would only be given if they had drawn up a business plan.

Objectives

● Appreciate the role and importance of a business plan in minimising the risk involved in setting up a business.

The purpose of the business plan

Chloe and Samir needed to borrow money from a bank to start their business. The banks they approached were interested in what the money would be used for. But they were also concerned about customers, costs, cash flow and the competition. They wanted to see a **business plan**. This is a document which puts together all the information showing how a business might survive in a competitive world.

The plan had two main functions. First, drawing up the plan would force Chloe and Samir to think about all aspects of their business and not just aspects like design and computers. It saved them from making costly mistakes about matters like insurance and tax, which they had not thought about. It would also force them to make a forecast of cash flow. All this research and forecasting will help reduce the risk of the business failing in its first couple of years of operation.

Second, it would help their bank manager, as well as others who would help them set up the business, to see whether the business stood a chance of being successful. After all, bank managers will only lend money to a business if they feel that it will be able to repay the loan with interest. If the business fails, the bank could lose the money it has loaned.

The business plan

Each bank gave Chloe and Samir a booklet about what should be included in a business plan. The details differed from bank to bank, but the main areas covered were resources, production, marketing and finance. Examples included:

- the name of the business, a brief history, its location, its legal structure (whether it is a limited company for instance) and who would be the owners;
- what equipment would be needed and its cost;
- what premises would be needed;
- who would be the suppliers to the business;
- the key personnel in the business including their position and salary;
- the product, whether it had been test marketed and what market research had been carried out;
- what production methods would be used;
- how the service would be marketed;
- what the total costs and revenues of the business would be;
- a cash flow forecast for the first 12 months;
- the sources of finance for the start-up of the business.

ResultsPlus
Watch Out!

Don't assume that every start-up business has a business plan. However, the evidence shows that businesses which do have a business plan are more likely to survive the first few years of trading than those which do not have a business plan.

edexcel ::: key terms

Business plan – a plan for the development of a business giving forecasts of items such as sales, costs and cash flow.

Chloe and Samir were now in a position to draw up their business plan. Part of this is shown in Figure 1. They found completing the business plan very difficult because it forced them to think of many areas of the business which they had not thought about at all. But once they had completed it, they showed it to Chloe's mother, Mary, who ran her own business. Mary evaluated the business plan. This meant she looked at it critically in two ways.

• She checked that all parts of the business plan had been completed.
• She thought about whether each part of the business plan was feasible. For example, could they really get that many orders in the first six months? Would the marketing make any impact?

ResultsPlus
Watch Out!

In a business plan, it is better for entrepreneurs to be cautious about the future prospects of the business. Then they can see what will happen if things do not go well. Can they survive even if sales are disappointing? Can they survive if costs are higher than might be expected?

ResultsPlus
Build Better Answers

Vicki McFarland and Wendy Jeffery have spotted the chance to be professional exam markers. There is some risk as work will usually only flow when students are taking major exams. Their research shows that they can make sufficient in the busy times to offset the quiet times. They decide to construct a business plan to try to think through their ideas.

Which **two** of the following are the most likely reasons to produce a business plan?

A   To show what good markers they are

B   To get support from the bank when cash flow might be slow

C   To show other people they could create a business plan

D   To show a bank their route to making a fortune

E   To convince the exam boards to give them more work

F   To help them monitor actual earnings against forecast earnings

Answer B and F

There is a number of choices available so first:

Think: What is the benefit of a business plan to Vicky and Wendy? What is not relevant to the plan?

Then: Dismiss the choices that are obviously wrong – that would be A. ■

Decide: You are left with B, C, D, E and F. You have narrowed down the options.

Go through these.

C is not relevant because it is not the purpose of a business plan.

D a business plan may help to show a bank how a business is expected to be a success but it is not a plan for making a fortune.

E relates to the quality of their marking not the quality of the business plan. ■

This leaves you with the most likely correct answers of B and F. They are both direct and practical uses of a business plan. Check to make sure your choices are right. ▲

82

Figure 1 – Part of the business plan of Skyfitters

The business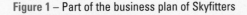

a **Name** Skyfitters Ltd

b **Address** 6 Ormskirk High St, Belfast.

c **Limited Company/Partnership/Sole Trader** Limited Company

d **What does your business do?** Supply and install shop fit-outs

e **Date you started trading** Hope to start Spring 2008
(**date you will start if you have a new business**)

f **Aims** To supply and install sell high quality shop fit-outs which
are both innovative in design and functional at a competitive price.

• **Limited company**	**Amount of capital**	**% of total**
Name *Chloe Simpson*	£1,000	50
Name *Samir Audard*	£1,000	50

Test yourself

1. Which **three** of the following would a start-up business be most likely to include in its business plan?

   Select **three** answers.

   A   A cash flow forecast
   B   A photograph of the business owners
   C   The location of the business
   D   How the product will be marketed
   E   The names of all its past customers
   F   The names of all its past suppliers
   G   The names and addresses of all employees

2. Which **two** of the following are most likely to be the reasons why the owners of a start-up business would draw up a business plan?

   Select **two** answers.

   A   To minimise the risks associated with starting a business
   B   To persuade a bank to lend money to the business
   C   To prove to Her Majesty's Revenue and Customs that the right amount of tax is being paid.
   D   To calculate the profit from the operations of the business to date
   E   To reduce the rent on the premises which the business is using

3. Drawing up a business plan helps reduce the risks of starting a business because

   A   banks like to see a business plan
   B   every business has a business plan
   C   a business plan encourages the entrepreneur to think about all aspects of the business
   D   profits can only be made if a business plan has been drawn up

   Select **one** answer.

Over to you

Kenton Travel Ltd was set up in 2009. It managed to achieve its first business aim, to make a profit of £5,000, in the first year. Kenton Travel is owned by Mohammad Ashraful and Atiur Rahman. The travel company provides small group tours to places like Vietnam, Cambodia and Indonesia.

Both Mohammad and Atiur are experienced travellers and wanted to mix business with pleasure when they first decided to start a business. They are both actively involved in leading tours and thoroughly enjoy what they do. Indeed, their success in business is partly down to their passion for travel that rubs off on their small group customers. However, planning before they started trading was also an important ingredient. The pair spent nearly two years researching destinations, accommodation, modes of travel and routes before drawing up a comprehensive business plan. They also went on courses to learn about marketing and accounting.

When Mohammad and Atiur drew up their cash flow forecast, they included the cost of setting up a website and advertising regularly in Sunday newspapers. They predicted that customers would spend an average of £3,000 each. In their cash flow forecast, they put in high figures for their costs and low figures for the sales. They hoped that making very cautious estimates would minimise the risk of their business failing within the first year due to lack of cash.

1. (a) What is meant by the term business plan? (1)

   (b) Give **three** examples of things that Mohammed and Atiur would have included in their business plan. (3)

2. Explain **two** ways in which Mohammad and Atiur did research which helped them to write their business plan before trading began. (8)

3. Mohammad and Atiur had a 'passion' for their business and drew up a business plan before they started. In your opinion, would this help to get rid of all the risks of setting up a new business? Justify your answer. (8)

18 Obtaining finance

Case Study

Business idea

Thousands of chefs dream about owning their own restaurant. But for Kiara Williams, it was not just a dream. It was a burning ambition. She trained as a chef in Cardiff and worked in some of the top hotels in London and Paris. She also worked in two famous restaurants – one in Oxford and one in London. Over a number of years she developed a wide range of cooking skills and a good understanding of the restaurant industry. She also managed to save up £20,000. Now she was ready to realise her ambition.

Objectives

- Explain the main sources of finance for a small business start-up.
- Understand long-term sources of finance, such as loans, personal savings, profit, venture capital and share capital in the context of a private limited company.
- Understand short-term sources of finance such as overdrafts and trade credit.

edexcel ::: key terms

Long-term finance – sources of money for businesses that are borrowed or invested typically for more than a year.

Short-term finance – sources of money for businesses that may have to be repaid either immediately or fairly quickly, such as an overdraft, usually within a year.

Share – a part ownership in a business; for example a shareholder owning 25 per cent of the shares of a business owns a quarter of the business.

Personal savings – money that has been set aside and not spent by individuals and households.

Share capital – the monetary value of a company which belongs to its shareholders; for example, if five people each invest £10,000 into a business, the share capital will be £50,000.

Shareholders – the owners of a company.

Getting started

Kiara drew up a business plan. She knew she would need to raise money to get started and run the business. She calculated she needed £100,000 to fit out the restaurant. Then she would need another £50,000 to cover her day-to-day expenses, such as

- wages for staff;
- utility bills such as electricity, water and gas;
- the rent on the premises;
- food ingredients for meals.

£150,000 was a lot of money to find. She was advised that most of it should come from **long-term finance** but some of it could be **short-term finance**. The difference is that long-term finance either never has to be repaid or it will be paid off over a long period of time. For small companies like Kiara's, this typically means up to five years although in some cases it can be up to 25 years. Short-term finance may have to be paid back over a much shorter period of time, up to one year's time.

Having taken advice, Kiara decided to set up a private limited company for her business. This reduced her risks if the business failed. It also meant that she could have several people investing in the company and becoming its shareholders or owners.

Long-term sources of finance

Kiara looked at three different types of long-term finance for her company.

Share capital One source of long-term capital for a start-up business is investors who will buy **shares** in the company. This means they take part-ownership of the business. Kiara was prepared to put all her £20,000 of **personal savings** into the business in this way. Who else could she find who might also invest in the business? For almost all small business start-ups, it is relations, friends or work colleagues who invest. Kiara talked to her father and he agreed to invest £75,000. Kiara also had a friend with whom she had worked in the past. He was prepared to put £25,000 into the business. So, in total she had found £120,000 of **share capital**. There would be three **shareholders** in the business. As part owners of the business, they would be entitled to a share of any profit made.

Very occasionally, entrepreneurs find professional investors who are willing to put money into a new company. These people or companies are called **venture capitalists**. They risk (or venture) their money (or capital) in the hope that the business will be a success. They are prepared to invest because they hope to be able to sell their share of the business at a large profit at a later date.

Loans Another source of long-term finance is a **loan**. Kiara persuaded her bank to lend her £30,000. Bank loans to businesses tend to be for periods up to 5 years. Banks prefer to have **security** (or **collateral** as it is sometimes called) for a loan. This is something of value, which the bank can sell if the business fails to repay the loan. Many small business owners offer their own home as security. If they don't repay the loan, the bank can force the house to be sold. The loan is then repaid from the proceeds of the sale. A loan is where property is offered as security is often called a **mortgage**. Banks loans have to be paid back with interest, usually in regular instalments at a fixed rate of interest, over a period of time. Kiara's bank loan was repayable over three years at £1,000 per month. However, some bank loans have rates of interest which can change as interest rates in the economy change. The costs of these loans can go down or they can go up.

Retained profit Once the business is up and running, it will hopefully make a profit. The profit belongs to the owners of the business. In Kiara's case, the profits belonged to the three shareholders. They could choose to take the profit out of the company as a **dividend** payment. This would be their reward for having invested in the company. They could agree to put the profit back into the business. It would then become **retained profit**. The money could be used to make the business financially stronger, for example by paying off debts. Or it could be used to finance expansion. Kiara hoped that retained profit within a couple of years could finance the opening of a second restaurant.

Leasing Some businesses use equipment or vehicles that can be rented from another business. This is an alternative to buying the equipment and borrowing the money to pay for it. Such rental agreements by businesses are called **leasing**. Often maintenance is including in the leasing agreement. Kiara's restaurant leases a van and also the computer systems that are used in the business. Repairs and servicing for both are paid for by the leasing company.

Grants Some start-up businesses are eligible for grants. Very small start-ups might get a grant from charities like the Prince's Trust. Grants are also available through government and the European Union particularly if the business is located in an area of high unemployment or where the government wants to encourage investment into the local economy. The great advantage of a grant is that the money does not have to be repaid and there is no interest either. However, in some cases, there are conditions attached to getting and using a grant. For example, the business might have to promise to provide jobs for a number of people.

Short-term sources of finance

Kiara's restaurant business needs to use a variety of short-term sources of finance.

Bank overdraft Kiara opened a bank account for the company to pay its day-to-day bills using cheques and bank cards. Money received from customers also was paid into the account. Kiara negotiated an **overdraft facility** of £2,000 with the bank. What this means is that the restaurant's account at the bank can go into

ResultsPlus
Watch Out!

Remember to make sure you understand the difference between the money needed to start-up a business and the money needed to run and expand the business when it is up and running. They are not always the same.

edexcel :::: key terms

Venture capitalist – an individual or company which buys shares in what they hope will be a fast growing company with a long-term view of selling the shares at a profit.

Loan – borrowing a sum of money which has to be repaid with interest over a period of time, such as 1-5 years.

Security (or collateral) – assets owned by a business which are used to guarantee repayments of a loan; if the business fails to pay off the loan, the lender can sell what has been offered as security.

Mortgage – a loan where property is used as security.

Dividend – a share of the profits of a company received by shareholders who own shares.

Retained profit – profit which is kept back in the business and used to pay for investment in the business.

Leasing – renting equipment or premises.

Overdraft facility – borrowing money from a bank by drawing more money than is actually in a current account. Interest is charged on the amount overdrawn.

the 'red' by up to £2,000: it can borrow up to £2,000 at any one time. The great advantage of an overdraft is that money is only borrowed when needed which cuts down on the interest that has to be paid on the borrowing. One day, the account might be in the 'black', with money in the bank. The next day, a cheque might have been paid out and the account slips into the red. For Kiara, the winter months were always better for business than the summer months. So in the summer, she tended to borrow money using her overdraft. An overdraft facility was one way she could manage her cash flow more effectively. A disadvantage of an overdraft is that the rate of interest can often be quite high, especially for small businesses.

Trade credit   When the restaurant orders supplies, its suppliers usually will allow a period of time before the supplies have to be paid. This is called trade credit. Typically, suppliers will give 30 days for a bill (called an invoice) to be paid. Even then, there is often no penalty if the bill is paid late. Trade credit is a form of short-term borrowing because goods and services do not have to be paid for immediately. For many businesses, the advantage of not having to pay for goods immediately is cancelled out by the fact that they have to offer their customers trade

credit too. So they get paid late for what they sell. But restaurants are lucky because most of their customers pay immediately.

Factoring   Some businesses raise finance through **factoring**. When a business supplies goods or services to other businesses, it typically has to give trade credit. This means it will often have to wait for at least 30 days for its invoices to be paid. A **factor** is a financial service company like a bank. It will pay the business typically 90 per cent of the value of invoices immediately. Instead of waiting 30 or more days, the business gets its money now. There is a price to be paid for this service. The factor charges a fee, which is like the interest on a loan. Not all businesses can use a factor even if they wanted to do so. Customers of Kiara's restaurant business, for example, pay immediately. So factoring is not a suitable method of finance for Kiara.

edexcel ⁞⁞⁞ key terms

Factoring – a source of finance where a business is able to receive cash immediately for the invoices it has issued from a **factor**, such as a bank, instead of waiting the typical 30 days to be paid.

ResultsPlus
Exam Question Report

5 (b) Lucy has a brother Dominic who is also a dentist. He is currently working as an associate dentist in another local practice but they are considering forming a partnership and opening an NHS dental practice in another town.

The purchase of a second dental practice required Lucy and Dominic to raise extra finance. Discuss the most suitable sources of finance they might have used for the purchase of the second dental practice. (12) (June 2007)

How students answered

Some students (23%) scored poorly (ie 0-4) on this question.

These answers gave incorrect or inappropriate sources of finance for a small business such as a dental practice, which was a partnership. An answer giving selling shares on the stock market would be incorrect. Some answers were not appropriate (i.e. a coffee morning or a raffle), whilst an overdraft is mainly a short-term source of finance and would not be used for the purchase of premises.

Most students (61%) gained good (between 5-8) marks on this question.

These answers considered the nature of a dental practice and the NHS. They discussed appropriate sources of finance, such as government grants, mortgages, loans and partners' own capital/retained finance.

Some students (16%) gained very good (ie 9-12) marks on this question.

These answers showed good judgement skills (the command word 'discuss' implies that evaluation is required). They chose appropriate sources of finance, gave clear reasons and judged why these sources were suitable for this type of business (i.e. a partnership which is a relatively small business) rather than other types of business.

Over to you

Perth Holdings Ltd is a Scottish-based company that makes drilling and other engineering equipment for the oil industry. It was set up in 2001 with £160,000 of share capital, a £40,000 bank loan and a £10,000 local authority grant. The shares were owned equally by Ella McDonald and Shane MacTaggart. Ella, who studied Business at Glasgow University, insisted that the business should be properly funded at the start. She knew that small businesses that lacked funding in the initial stages often struggled. The company rents a factory unit on an industrial estate and leases about 80 per cent of its machinery and equipment.

The company has done well since starting up. The rising oil price has resulted in a boom in oil exploration and Perth Holdings has benefited. Most of the company's recent growth has been funded through retained profit. This has avoided the need to increase the amount borrowed through loans significantly.

In 2008, the price of oil reached a record high and the factory was running at full capacity. Ella and Shane decided it was time to move to larger premises and cash in on the continuing boom. They drew up a business plan for expansion. They calculated they would need to raise £200,000 to make the move and update their technology. A bank agreed to loan them all the money.

1. Analyse **two** differences between '£160,000 of share capital' and a '£40,000 bank loan'. (6)

2. Explain **two** reasons why a company like Perth Holdings would choose to lease machinery and equipment rather than buying it outright. (6)

3. Perth Holdings Ltd could borrow the £200,000 from a bank or seek investment from a venture capitalist to help it expand. In your opinion, which would be the better option for Perth Holdings Ltd to fund its expansion? (8)

Test yourself

1. Which **two** of the following are examples of long-term finance for a high street chain of fashion shops? Select **two** answers.

   A *An overdraft*
   B *Trade credit*
   C *A three year bank loan*
   D *New shares*
   E *A Christmas sale*

2. On which **one** of the following would a business pay interest? Select **one** answer.

   A *A bank loan*
   B *Shares*
   C *Personal savings*
   D *Retained profit*

3. Which **one** of the following is most likely to be an example of a type of finance where the lender can demand immediate repayment from a business which has borrowed the money?

   A *An overdraft*
   B *A share*
   C *A bank loan*
   D *Retained profit*

ResultsPlus
Watch Out!

The typical business start-up needs a mix of both long-term and short-term finance. It needs long-term finance to pay for all the costs of setting up and then running the business. It needs short-term finance to cope with changing cash flows through the business. For instance, many businesses see sales peak in the run up to Christmas. They use short-term finance to get them through this period when costs tend to be high.

ResultsPlus
Watch Out!

Many start-up businesses fail because they do not have enough long-term finance. Then either they cannot get enough short-term finance to run the business and have to stop trading. Or they get into financial difficulties: banks and other businesses then ask for what they are owed to be paid immediately which the business cannot do. So the business collapses owing money.

In this topic you have learned about: cash flow and its role in a new business, objectives and how they provide a focus for a new business when starting up, obtaining suitable finance to get the business going, qualities needed by the entrepreneur to get the business up and running, understanding how external influences can affect small businesses and estimating revenue and costs and how to calculate profit or loss.

You should know...

- ☐ A financial objective is one set by the entrepreneur involving money and will be quantitative and easy to measure.

- ☐ A non-financial objective is one set by the entrepreneur which will be more personal to her or him and will be qualitative. Only the entrepreneur really knows if this has been achieved.

- ☐ An entrepreneur is someone who is prepared to take a risk on something they have researched, planned and in which they believe.

- ☐ Entrepreneurs need the personal skills of drive and leadership.

- ☐ Entrepreneurs need the technical skills of thorough research and good financial planning.

- ☐ Cash flow is a record of the money flowing into and out of a business.

- ☐ More money flowing into the business than out of it is called a 'surplus'.

- ☐ More money flowing out of a business than in is called a 'shortfall'.

- ☐ A cash flow forecast is only an estimate. An entrepreneur uses it to check with what actually happens to see if the planning and research were correct.

- ☐ A cash flow statement is used to show what actually happened and provides the means to make a comparison.

- ☐ Revenue is the income a business receives from its customers. It is found by multiplying price charged by the number of items sold.

- ☐ Price is what the customer pays the business for something the customer buys. It is what has to be given up to acquire a good or service in exchange.

- ☐ Cost is what the business pays for resources such as labour, equipment, buildings, materials and so on, which are needed to produce goods and services.

- ☐ If revenue is higher than cost over a period of time this gives the business a profit.

- ☐ If costs are higher than revenue over a given time, this gives the business a loss.

- ☐ Long-term finance is used for big purchases that last a long time and can be used over and over again such as buildings or expensive equipment and machinery.

- ☐ Short-term finance is for smaller immediate purchases that are more irregular such as stock.

Support activity

To help understand cash flow students should think about their own cash flow in a week.

Make a list of the different ways they receive cash and the amounts they receive. Add up the totals.

Make a list of the different ways they pay out cash and the amounts they pay out. Add up the totals.

Calculate their net cash flow – the amount they receive minus the amount they pay.

Consider how any money left over might be used and when it would be used.

Consider what they might do if they did not have enough cash to pay for the things they wanted to buy.

Stretch activity

To challenge yourself to see if you can manage cash flow over a period of a year, visit **http://www.bized.co.uk/learn/business/accounting/cashflow/simulation/index.htm** - Biz/ed's Cash Flow Simulation game.

Here you will be presented with a scenario and a cash flow forecast for a small business. You can test your understanding

and ability to react to changes in the business to see if you can survive the year. Sound easy? Bear in mind that over 80% of those who attempt this end up being forced to close so it is a real challenge, as is the case with real businesses, to manage cash flow carefully.

(a) Sourav has opened a cycle shop in Nottingham. He is preparing a cash flow forecast for the next six months from July to the end of the year. In July the business has an opening balance of £50,000. In July total receipts are £45,000 and total payments are £120,000.

(i) What is meant by the term 'cash flow'? (1)

(ii) Explain why the cycle shop has a cash flow problem. (3)

Think: What is cash flow? How does cash flow work? What is the cash flow in this scenario? What is the problem facing the business?

Student answer	Examiner comment	Build a better answer
(i) Cash flow is money in and out of a business.	A basic answer that has the idea but which does not use appropriate terminology.	Use phrases like 'money flowing in and out of a business' and state what the money flowing in and out represents. For example, '…money flowing in is as a result of the revenues received from sales whereas the money flowing out is the payments for raw materials, stock and overheads that make up the cost of production'.
(ii) The cycle shop has a cash flow problem because in July money flowing out is higher than money flowing in. The business has a negative net cash flow of -£75,000. There is not enough in the business at the start of January to cover this.	A good answer that identifies the amount of the cash flowing in and out of the business and which works out the negative cash flow. The problem is then identified – the business does not have enough cash to pay for the outgoings.	Start with a clear statement of the problem in July, showing working out. For example, 'In July total payments (£120,000) are higher than total receipts (£45,000) The net cash flow is, therefore, negative, (-£75,000)'. Then relate the negative cash flow to the opening balance to show that the business does not have enough cash to be able to finance its operations. For example, 'The opening balance is £50,000 so this means the closing balance is -£25,000. This presents the business with a problem because it does not have the cash to buy stock'.

Practice Exam Questions

Anne Milford knew from her work in the fashion world that there was a demand for up-market hampers for glamorous picnics and parties. Even though she had not been involved in this type of business, she felt her contacts would give her the start she needed.

She did some research locally and found there were no competitors. However, she did not carry out in-depth research about sales beyond her contacts. She was not aware of sales trends, what prices were charged or even whether such businesses existed. She believed the quality of the product, her reputation, determination, self-belief and word of mouth would be enough to generate sales and meet her objectives of being rich and famous. She had £20,000 of her own to start the business, which she would run from the house that she owned in Sunderland. Apart from some utility bills, such as gas, electricity, telephone and water, accountants' fees and raw material costs, Anne thought she would have no other overheads. This led her to believe the objective of being rich would happen relatively easily.

From her research Anne knew that she would need some extra finance to start her business. She asked her friends Toni and Linda if they would like to invest. They looked at the ideas which she had

set out in a business plan. As a result of looking at the plan they decided not to invest. Anne turned to her bank, as her personal savings were not enough. The bank told her that her business plan was not detailed enough and that she needed to think about her financial projections more carefully. They also wanted to see a cash flow forecast and some budgets. Anne had been happier drawing up the marketing part of the plan than the financial part.

(a) Which **two** of the following costs will Anne **not** have to pay? (2)

A Staff wages   D Rent
B Raw materials   E Heating
C Electricity   F Water

(b) Anne sees herself as an entrepreneur. Describe two qualities she will need to succeed in her business venture. (4)

(c) Do you think that you would invest in Anne's business? Justify your answer. (6)

Topic 1.4: Making the start-up effective

Case study

Jason Livermore had worked in sports centres for a number of years. At 28 he was feeling frustrated and wanted to take on more responsibility. He noticed that at certain times of the day a certain type of customer visited the centres. They were either parents who looked after children or business people who appeared to have limited time. He talked to these customers and found that they would like a personal trainer who could tailor fitness programmes to their needs.

Topic overview

This topic considers the practicalities of making a business idea happen. What are the objectives in setting up? What are the qualities of a successful entrepreneur? How will estimates of revenues, costs, profits and cash flow fit into the business plan? What sources of finance are available to a start-up business?

That was four years ago. He set up his own business having rented rooms in a town centre and operated as a fitness centre specialising in offering tailor made personal fitness programmes. The marketing mix for the new business was simple. He charged a competitive price for his programmes compared to local sports and fitness centres. His promotion strategy was to maintain contact with customers through phone calls and emails. At regular intervals he would meet with his customers to check that the programme was to their satisfaction. At the same time, he would ask whether there were any other people they knew who would be interested in his services. As for 'place' in the marketing mix, he dealt directly with customers who were all in the local area, within 15 miles of his centre.

For the first couple of years, Jason operated as a sole trader. As the number of customers expanded he moved to new premises. Having taken advice, Jason decided to change the ownership and became a private limited company to reduce risks should the business not do well in the future. By this stage, he was employing four workers and had registered to pay VAT six months previously. His company was now responsible for paying VAT, National Insurance contributions and corporation tax. He and his workers also paid income tax.

Two years further on and Jason bought new machinery because of the demand for his services. He also expanded the services to include lifestyle advice and yoga. He put his success down to excellent customer service. His programmes suited his customers' needs. He knew his customers were satisfied because of the amount of repeat business he did. Nearly all customers renewed their membership each year.

Buying the new machines meant recruiting more staff. With skilled workers in short supply, he did not get many applications from his adverts. He was also aware that he wanted to recruit staff that would be well motivated and have a positive attitude to work.

Dealing with all the legal aspects of running a business was difficult. For a start, there was all the employment legislation relating to discrimination, recruitment and redundancy. However, he felt that, if he treated his staff fairly, they would be well motivated and he would keep within the law.

1. Explain why customers and customer satisfaction are so important for Jason's business.
2. Why does setting up a private limited company reduce risk compared to operating as a sole trader?
3. What could be the problems for Jason's business if his staff were not well motivated?
4. Should Jason spend more on promoting his business to customers? Justify your answer.

What will I learn?

Customer focus Why must a business anticipate, identify and meet customer needs if it is to be successful?

The marketing mix Why are price, product, promotion and place important elements of the marketing mix? Why do different businesses place different emphasis on the elements of the marketing mix? How can the marketing mix can be amended to meet changing consumer needs?

The importance of limited liability What is the principle of limited and unlimited liability? Why does liability have implications for choice on the status of the business? What are the differences between sole trade and private limited company status?

Start-up legal and tax issues Why is establishing a unique trading and business name important? Why is it necessary to keep careful business records? What are the implications of VAT, income tax, National Insurance and Corporation Tax for the business?

Effective on-time delivery and customer satisfaction Why is fulfilling customer orders accurately and on-time and dealing with complaints important for effective customer service? Why is customer satisfaction important to the success of a business? Why is repeat purchase important for a business?

Recruiting, training and motivating staff What are the basic processes involved in recruiting staff to work in a small business? Is skill more important than attitude when it comes to recruiting and training staff? Why is treating staff fairly important? What impact does employment legislation, for example relating to age, sex, race and disability discrimination, have on a business?

How will I be assessed?

Unit 1 A forty-five minute written examination of multiple choice and objective test questions.

Unit 2 Research and investigate a real life business from a choice of five tasks and write up the results under controlled assessment conditions.

Unit 6 A forty-five minute written examination of multiple choice, objective test and extended answer questions.

19 Customer focus and the marketing mix

92

Case Study

Fahmida Nabi is in her final year of university. She has been studying for the past two and half years for a degree in Silversmithing, Goldsmithing and Jewellery. At the end of her course, she would like to set up in business making original pieces of jewellery. However, she has a lot of choices to make about the direction of her business.

Objectives

● Understand that any business needs customers to survive.

● Appreciate that knowing who and how many customers might be interested in buying products from the business is important.

● Understand that a business must anticipate, identify and meet customer needs if it is to be successful.

● Understand that a business will have to consider its price, the product itself, how to make customers aware of the product (promotion) and how to get the product to the consumer (place) as important elements in meeting customer needs.

● Understand that different businesses will place different emphasis on the elements of the mix and that the mix can be amended to meet changing consumer needs.

Customer focus

A business can only survive if it has customers. A business must have enough customers willing to pay a high enough price for it to cover its costs and make a profit. Focusing on what the customer wants is vital to most businesses. Also, successful businesses are often ones that are able to anticipate changes in customer needs.

For a small or start-up business, customer focus is essential if it wants to make the business a success. Entrepreneurs may think they have a good idea for a product but there have to be customers willing to pay money if the idea is to become a business.

Identifying needs Businesses must understand what their customers want from a product. Fahmida knows that there are already many successful businesses in the jewellery trade. Some businesses make jewellery which is a fun, impulse (or spur of the moment) purchase. This sort of jewellery tends to be cheap and colourful. It is the sort of jewellery you might buy on a Saturday afternoon shopping expedition when you are looking for clothes or shoes. Other businesses make more expensive jewellery designed to be a one-off purchase. It might be an engagement ring or wedding ring for example. This sort of jewellery satisfies a completely different customer need. It is about status, prestige and showing commitment.

Anticipating needs Jewellery is part of the wider fashion industry. As with clothes, fashion in jewellery changes over time. A successful business must understand what its customers want in advance. If Fahmida makes jewellery that was fashionable ten years ago but is no longer fashionable today, she will not do very well. For Fahmida to succeed, she must be at the forefront of fashion. She has to be able to try to understand how fashions change and how this might affect customer wants and needs.

Meeting customer needs Identifying and anticipating customer needs is not enough. Businesses then have to meet those needs. If the market wants smart but inexpensive jewellery, Fahmida must supply those products. Quality will be important whatever the price charged. If her customers buy a £2 necklace, they will not expect it to be made with gold and diamonds. But they will expect the clasp that closes the necklace to work. It will not meet customer needs if it has to be thrown away broken after being worn once.

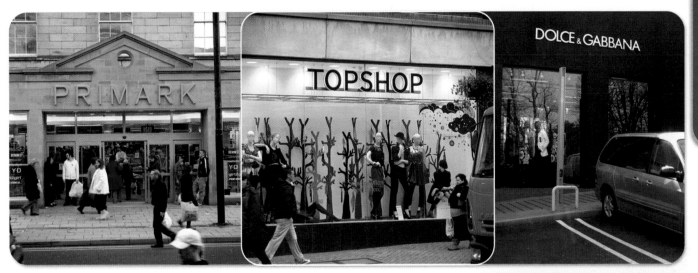

The marketing mix of Primark, Topshop and Dolce & Gabbana are likely to be different

The marketing mix

Any business must consider the **marketing mix**. This is the combination of factors that helps a business sell its products. There are four parts to the marketing mix: price, product, promotion and place. These are often called the '4 Ps' because each word starts with a P.

Price The **price** of a product must reflect the value that customers place on the product. Fahmida could produce low cost costume jewellery made from cheap materials. Customers might be happy to buy this but only at a low price. Equally, Fahmida could produce high cost jewellery made from expensive materials, such as gold and diamonds, with a high level of quality. The price could then be high to reflect what customers are prepared to pay for this quality. Price, quality and how customers perceive the product are all interlinked. Price is also important for Fahmida because it will affect how much she earns from her work. Her business will only be successful if the price she charges allows her to make a profit.

Product The **product** sold must meet customer needs. For Fahmida, this means identifying into which segment of the market she plans to sell. Will it be cheap and cheerful jewellery aimed at a mass market? Will it be expensive hand crafted jewellery with each piece costing hundreds or thousands of pounds? Once in production, she must ensure that her product is attractive and well made for the price. Other businesses have to make sure that the product meets customer needs by doing what it says it will do or having appropriate technical specifications. The look and design of a product might be important factors in consumers' decisions about buying it.

Promotion Customers need to know that a product exists and is available for purchase. **Promotion** is partly about giving them knowledge about the product: making them aware that it exists. It is also about persuading them that they want to buy the product. Promotion includes advertising, printed brochures, mailing leaflets to customers (direct mail), sales promotions like two for one offers or free gifts, and sponsorship. For Fahmida, it is about getting her jewellery noticed by customers. She could not afford to advertise on television. However, she could afford to have a catalogue printed and sent to possible customers. If she opened a jewellery shop, she might consider advertising in her local newspaper.

ResultsPlus
Watch Out!

In some industries, the needs of customers change very quickly. In fashion retailing, for example, there are new styles and trends every season. In other industries, the needs of customers change very slowly. A farmer growing sprouts or cabbages is not operating in a fast changing customer environment. Think very carefully about what you write in a question about customer needs. You do not want to be saying that farmers should change their milk or their cabbages or their potatoes every few months to satisfy customer needs.

edexcel key terms

Marketing mix – the combination of factors which help the business to take into account customer needs when selling a product - usually summarised as the 4 Ps, which are price, product, promotion and place.

Price – the amount of money customers have to give up to acquire a product.

Product – a good or service produced by a business or organisation and made available to customers for consumption.

Promotion – communication between the business and customer, making the customer aware that the product is for sale, telling or explaining to them what is the product, making the customers aware of how the product will meet the customers' needs and persuading them to buy it for the first time or again.

94

Place Place is about having a product available to customers where they want it, when they want it. Having Christmas turkeys on sale in Scotland in July for sale to customers in London is bad marketing. Fahmida faces difficult decisions about place. How can she get her jewellery to customers? Should she sell to specialist jewellery shops? Should she try to get products stocked by supermarkets such as Tesco or clothes retailers like Primark or TopShop? Could she sell directly to customers through mail order or over the Internet? Could she have a market stall or open her own shop and if so, where should it be? Then she has to think of timing. Are there periods of peak demand for jewellery during the year? Is it like many products where sales peak at Christmas?

Differences in the marketing mix

The marketing mix is different for each business and for each industry. So the marketing mix for cars is different from that for cornflakes or that for jewellery. Fahmida could not afford to advertise on television. This is so expensive that it can

only be afforded by large companies selling branded products like cars, alcoholic drink or branded food products. However, she could afford to run a website. Alternatively, she could sell her jewellery on eBay, an Internet auction site.

Her business will be very different depending on whether she produces high quality, expensive jewellery or cheap jewellery. In the same way, the marketing mix for fashion houses like Yves St Laurent or Dolce & Gabbana is different from that of Marks & Spencer, TopShop or Primark. A much larger proportion of the cost of a garment bought at Dolce & Gabbana is spent on promotion than of a garment bought from TopShop.

Fahmida has to think carefully about her marketing mix. Say she chooses to make low cost, cheap but fashionable jewellery. Her price then has to be relatively low to reflect the 'throw away' nature of the product. The product has to look fashionable but because the price consumers are prepared to pay is low the materials she uses will have to be inexpensive if she is to make a profit on her sales. She might choose to produce leaflets to promote her jewellery and give them to younger people. As for 'place', she might consider setting up a market stall in a city centre where lots of young people shop - the sort of people who are most likely to buy her jewellery. She may feel that, in addition, she could sell her jewellery on a website like eBay.

The decisions Fahmida makes on the four elements of the mix might be very different from those made by businesses outside the fashion world, such as a children's entertainer or a landscape gardener. Large businesses will have a very different marketing mix from small businesses, if only because they have more money and so more options. However, they all have one thing in common - they must focus on what the customer wants to be successful.

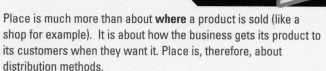

Results Plus
Watch Out!

Place is much more than about **where** a product is sold (like a shop for example). It is about how the business gets its product to its customers when they want it. Place is, therefore, about distribution methods.

edexcel ::: key terms

Place – the way in which a product is distributed - how it gets from the producer to the consumer.

Test yourself

1. Which **two** of the following would be essential elements of customer focus for a business?

   A *Anticipating customer needs*
   B *Ordering stocks of raw materials*
   C *Meeting customer needs*
   D *Paying consumer tax*
   E *Paying workers*

   Select **two** answers.

2. Which **two** of the following would be part of the marketing mix for a business?

   A *Production*
   B *Place*
   C *Stocks*
   D *Price*
   E *Workers*

   Select **two** answers.

3. Which **two** of the following would be the **most likely** examples of promotion?

   A *Stocks*
   B *Two for one offers*
   C *Production*
   D *Quality*
   E *Advertising*

   Select **two** answers.

Over to you

Hannah Abruquah works in the design department for a designer clothes manufacturing business. However, she has plans to set up her own business. The business will manufacture clothes specially designed by Hannah for women aged 20-40 years who are sized 16 and above. Hannah's friends and family have always told her how frustrated they are that so many fashion shops do not stock larger sizes for fashion conscious women. They said 'You should really do something about this'. She wants her clothes to be exciting, fashionable but reasonably priced. Her range will include pieces suitable to wear to go to work at the office, or for a night out with friends.

Working for an existing business, Hannah knows that one of her biggest problems will be persuading shops to buy her collection of clothes. If she cannot get her clothes into shops, she will not be able to get her 20-40 year old target market to buy her clothes. Setting up a website to sell directly to customers is one way round the problem. However, this probably will not give enough sales to make her business a success. She will have to persuade shops and boutiques to stock her clothes. To do this, she will have to take a stand at the regular trade fairs that are visited by the owners of independent clothes retailers where they choose and buy their stock. Promotion would also mean sending out brochures and leaflets to shops that might consider buying her products. Advertisements in selected magazines might also be affordable.

1. Explain how each **one** of the following elements of the marketing mix could contribute to the success of Hannah's future business:
   (a) price; (3)
   (b) product; (3)
   (c) promotion; (3)
   (d) place. (3)
2. (i) What is meant by 'customer focus'? (1)
   (ii) Explain why customer focus will be important to Hannah's business. (3)
3. 'The marketing mix for a shop which sold fashion clothes in larger sizes would be very different from the marketing mix for Hannah's business.' Do you agree with this? Justify your answer. (6)

ResultsPlus
Build Better Answers

(a) Draw **four** lines to match the following with the appropriate element of the marketing mix.

(i)	**Charging the same as the competition**	**A Price**
(ii)	**New improved version**	**B Product**
(iii)	**Stamps available online**	**C Promotion**
(iv)	**In-store display**	**D Place**
(v)	**Free gift**	**E Promotion**

Answer
(i) - A   (iv) - C or E
(ii) - B   (v) - C or E
(iii) - D

Technique: You have 4 Ps of the marketing mix (price, promotion, product and place) but 5 elements. This means that two of the elements relate to just **one** of the marketing mix (promotion) which is included twice, in C and E.

Think: what are the features of the 4Ps of the marketing mix?

Then: decide which elements clearly relate to parts of the marketing mix.

Decide:

'Charging' is about **price**. So (i) = A

A new 'version' is about the **product**. So (ii) = B

Stamps available 'online' is about **where** the stamps are available, which relates to **place** in the marketing mix. So (iii) = D.

This leaves 'Instore displays' and 'Free gifts' as examples of promotions - both are ways in which consumer awareness of a product is increased. So either (iv) = C and (v) = E or (iv) = E and (v) = C.

20 The importance of limited liability

Case Study

Rich Perry is a national record plugger. Record companies and their artists, like music bands or solo singers, want to get their music played on radio stations such as Radio 1` and Kiss. Not only do they get a royalty fee every time their music is played, but it is free publicity for the artist. They are then likely to sell more CDs and more people will come and hear them play live at gigs. Rich Perry uses his knowledge of the music industry to 'plug' or promote the artists he represents to music stations.

Objectives

● Explain the principle of limited and unlimited liability.

● Understand how the amount that could be lost in the event of business failure influences the choice of the type of business ownership.

● Appreciate the differences between sole trader and private limited company status.

edexcel ::: key terms

Sole trader (or Sole proprietor) – the only owner of a business which has unlimited liability.

Unlimited liability – a legal obligation on the owner of a business to settle (pay off) all debts of the business. In law, there is no distinction between what the business owes and owns and what the business owner owes and owns.

Limited liability – when shareholders of a company are not personally liable for the debts of the company: the most they can lose is the value of their investment in the shares of the company.

Unlimited liability and being a sole trader

Rich Perry is a **sole trader** (or **sole proprietor**). This means he is the only owner of his business. There are nearly 4 million sole traders in the UK today. Sole traders, for example, might be farmers, plumbers, electricians or shop owners.

Sole traders have **unlimited liability**. The word 'liability' here means being legally responsible for debts. 'Unlimited' means there is no limit to this responsibility to pay debts. So sole traders are completely responsible for paying all the debts of their business.

One feature of unlimited liability is that there is no legal difference between their own personal finances and the finances of the business. The owner and the business are seen as one and the same thing. For example, Rich Perry might use his credit card to pay for a meal at a restaurant. He is personally responsible for paying the credit card bill whether he went to the restaurant with friends, or he was taking one of his clients out to lunch for business purposes.

This could be very important if Rich Perry were to borrow money to buy premises for his business. Say he borrowed £300,000 to buy an office. He would be personally responsible for paying back the loan. If he could not afford the repayments, then he could be forced to sell his house to repay the loan.

Unlimited liability therefore creates personal risk for sole traders. If their business does badly and makes a loss, the sole trader is personally responsible for all the debts of the business.

However, most business start-ups choose to become sole traders. This is because it is easy to set up and easy to run compared to other forms of business ownership. Being a sole trader means that someone like Rich Perry can own their business. Sole traders do not have to share ownership of the business with anyone else. All the profits of the business go to the sole trader. So when Rich Perry is successful in his business, he gets all the rewards. He does not have to share these with anyone else. A sole trader also has complete control of the business.

Limited liability and private limited companies

Rich Perry could have chosen to make his business into a **private limited company**. Owners of this type of business have **limited liability**. This means that the owners of the business are only partly responsible for repaying any debts of the business. It also means that the finances of the business are legally separate from the finances of the owners of the business.

Businesses that have limited liability are called companies in the UK. The owners of a company are called **shareholders**. There must be at least one shareholder in a private limited company. Shareholders have limited liability. This means that the personal finances of the shareholders are completely separate from those of the company. If the company gets into financial difficulties, the shareholders can lose what they invested in the shares of the company in the first place. But this is the limit of their liability. They are not personally liable for any more of the debts of the company. If the company is forced to close but owes money to other businesses such as banks, the shareholders cannot be forced, for example, to sell their homes to pay off those debts.

Say someone set up a company and invested £10,000 in the shares of the company along with another investor. The company buys an office costing £300,000. This is financed by a loan of £300,000 from a bank. The company then does very badly and is forced to close. Neither of the two shareholders would be responsible for paying any of the £300,000 or any other debts of the company. The bank could sell the office to try and get back its money. However, it could not force either of the shareholders to sell their own personal possessions like a house. The most the two investors could lose is the £10,000 they each put into the company at the start.

Differences between private limited companies and sole traders

There is a number of differences between private limited companies and sole traders.

Risk Limited liability means that owning a company is less risky than being a sole trader. If things go badly for a limited liability company, the owners can only lose the value of their shares in the company. If things go badly for sole traders, they can at worst lose everything they own including their personnel assets like a house.

Control Control of the typical private limited company depends on the proportion of shares owned by a shareholder. Say Rich Perry owned a company and had 80 per cent of the shares. The other 20 per cent was owned by a friend. Rich Perry would then control the company because he would have 80 per cent of the votes at any shareholders' meeting. However, if Rich Perry had 40 per cent of the shares and two friends had 30 per cent each, no one shareholder would control the company. In contrast, control of a sole trader would be in the hands of the owner and no-one else.

Profits Profits of a company are also typically distributed according to the proportion of shares owned. If a shareholder owns 80 per cent of the shares, then the shareholder gets 80 per cent of any profit paid out to the owners. With sole traders, because they are the only owners of their business, they get all the profits.

Privacy Private limited companies must, by law, file their accounts each year with an agency of government called Companies House. Their accounts are a record of the value of their sales, their costs and their profits for a 12 month period. These accounts can then be seen by anyone who asks and pays a small fee to Companies House to see them. In comparison, no private individual or business has a right to see the accounts of a sole trader. So being a sole trader gives someone like Rich Perry more privacy than being a limited company.

ResultsPlus
Watch Out!

Being a shareholder in a limited company reduces risks compared to being a sole trader but it does not get rid of all risks. If you have invested £100,000 in the shares of a limited company, you stand to lose all the £100,000 if the company fails and has to be closed. However, unlike with a sole trader, you would not be forced to pay any outstanding debts of the company.

ResultsPlus
Watch Out!

Remember that a sole trader has a single owner but may employ many people.

edexcel ::: **key terms**

Companies – businesses whose shareholders have limited liability.

Test yourself

1. A shareholder in a private limited company has

   A *unlimited liability*
   B *an entitlement to a share of the profits of the company*
   C *complete control of the company*
   D *complete privacy about the financial affairs of the company*

   Select **one** answer.

2. A sole trader faces more risk than a shareholder in a company because of

   A *changes in profits*
   B *lack of control of the business*
   C *unlimited liability*
   D *lack of privacy*

   Select **one** answer.

3. Alfie Parkes is a sole trader who works as a gardener. His business has performed very poorly and it has run up debts of £50,000. Alfie has invested £75,000 in the business overall and has used his house as security for a loan of £30,000. His house is worth £200,000. He owes £20,000 to suppliers. How much of the debts run up by his business is Alfie responsible for paying himself if the business were to close? Select **one** answer.

   A *£20,000*
   B *£50,000*
   C *£75,000*
   D *£30,000*

   Select **one** answer.

ResultsPlus
Exam Question Report

3 (b) (ii) Why do you think limited liability is seen as a benefit to shareholders? (4) (June 2006)

How students answered

Most students (68%) scored poorly (ie 0-1) on this question. These answers demonstrated lack of depth of knowledge or did not make a judgement. When a question starts with 'why do you think' it means some judgement is required. They may have simply stated that limited liability gives protection to shareholders without going into more detail about why it was a benefit.

Some students (26%) gained good (ie 2-3) marks on this question. These answers would have explained that limited

liability means that only investments in the business are lost. Some limited judgement might have been made, such as reduced risk.

Few students (6%) gained very good (ie 4) marks on this question. These answers would have included an explanation and a judgement. For example, 'If the business goes bust the shareholders only lose the amount of their investment not their personal possessions. This encourages them to invest. Having limited liability is therefore less risky for investors.'

Over to you

Edward and Reece Westwick, two brothers, worked for a number of building companies before deciding to set up their own business as scaffolders. Health and safety laws today mean that scaffolding is needed for most building jobs above first floor height level. So they expected to get plenty of work from builders needing scaffolding to be put up.

They have to decide what type of business they would form. Edward was the older brother and had more experience. They could have agreed to set up as a sole trader with Edward as the owner and Reece as an employee. However, Reece was not keen on simply being an employee. He wanted to be the joint owner of a business. So they are probably going to set up a private limited company. They would both be shareholders,

owning half the company each. Setting up a private limited company would also have the advantage that it would reduce risks if the business did not do as well as they hoped.

1. Explain, using the Westwick brothers as an example, what is meant by (a) limited companies and (b) shareholders. (6)
2. Why might setting up a limited company reduce risks for the two brothers? (3)
3. Consider **two** possible advantages for the two brothers of Edward becoming a sole trader and employing Reece, rather than setting up a limited company and both being shareholders. (6)

Test yourself

1. Which **two** of the following are the best examples of effective customer service?

   A   *Selling large quantities to customers*
   B   *Fulfilling customer orders accurately*
   C   *Holding a Christmas sale to dispose of stock*
   D   *Dealing promptly with customer complaints*
   E   *Having no repeat purchases*

   Select **two** answers.

2. Hay's is a small pizza business offering either take-away pizza from its shop or a pizza delivery service.

   Select **two** answer.

   On-time delivery is important to the success of the business because

   A   *otherwise stocks would be too low*
   B   *it creates more jobs*
   C   *it helps to improve cash flow*
   D   *it leads to customer satisfaction*

3. Witton Industrial Ceramics is a business that manufactures and sells pottery.

   Select **two** answer.

   Repeat purchases from customers are most likely to be important to the success of Witton Industrial Ceramics because they increase

   A   *fixed costs*
   B   *prices*
   C   *sales turnover*
   D   *venture capital*

ResultsPlus
Build Better Answers

Jilly takes great pride in the level of customer service at her business. She runs a small hairdressing salon for men and women. There is a great deal of competition in her immediate area and she relies on clients returning to the salon as well as attracting new customers.

(a) (i) Identify **one** way in which a business such as Jilly's could improve customer service. (1)

(ii) Explain how the way you have identified in (i) above could benefit Jilly's business. (3)

Think: Who are the customers of a small hairdressers? What is customer service? What services would customers at such a business expect to receive? What does a business receive in return for these services?

■ **Basic** Identifies one method of improving customer service (1) - the experience that a customer gets when dealing with a business and the extent to which that experience meets and exceeds customer needs and expectations. (1)

● **Good** Identifies one method of improving customer service - the experience that a customer gets when dealing with a business and the extent to which that experience meets and exceeds customer needs and expectations. (1) Explains that good service could mean that customers are satisfied. This could lead to customer loyalty and repeat business. (1) It might also attract new customers. (1)

▲ **Excellent** Identifies one method of improving customer service - the experience that a customer gets when dealing with a business and the extent to which that experience meets and exceeds customer needs and expectations. (1). Explains that, in a highly competitive market, good service could make the difference between the success of Jilly's business and those of her rivals. This would help to develop brand loyalty and lead to repeat business. (1) Word of mouth and a good reputation mean that it could possibly attract new customers, especially when the business is small. (1) Higher customer spending would increase sales revenue and could lead to higher profits. (1)

Over to you

Libby Headon trained as a plumber ten years ago and set up her own plumbing business. Although some of her work is for building companies, most of her time is spent dealing with household repairs.

Libby's business has three unique selling points. First, the quality of her work is excellent. Second, her charges are very reasonable. Third, she is a woman. Many female customers say they prefer having a woman doing repairs in their house. They feel safer and they trust the quality of the work.

Libby has a tried and tested formula when someone rings her up. She arranges when she can do the work and tells the customer what she charges for a call out and the rate per hour of work. If on the day of the appointment she is running late, she always lets her clients know by telephoning them. Once at the customer's house, she gives a quote for the work. Once the work is completed, she gives the customer three of her business cards. One is for them to keep in case they need to

contact her. The other two she asks her customers to give to friends or relations in case they should ever need a plumber. If there is ever any problem with the work she has done, she calls back as quickly as possible to fix it.

Many plumbers pay to advertise in publications like Yellow Pages. Libby Headon has not spent any money on advertising for the past eight years. All her work comes from previous customers or through word of mouth recommendations.

1. Explain the importance of (a) quality of work and (b) dealing with complaints to the success of Libby Headon's business. (6)

2. How does repeat business contribute to the success of Libby's business? (3)

3. 'A successful plumbing business is all about customer service'. Do you agree with this statement? Justify your answer. (6)

Know Zone: Topic 1.4
Making the start-up effective

In this topic you have learned about: customer needs before, during and after selling to ensure progress and repeat sales, liability and how this differs between a sole trader and a private limited company, unique trading names and their role when starting up a business, taxation and how it affects business, the emphasis placed on the elements of the marketing mix with different products recruitment and the aspects a business needs to consider to get it right.

You should know...

- ☐ Meeting customer needs are essential to survive and be successful for a business. There are three stages in getting this right - anticipate, identify and meet the needs, often via market research.

- ☐ The marketing mix, the 4Ps, is price (types), product, promotion (where, is it suitable?), place (how to get the product to the customer).

- ☐ The emphasis on elements of the marketing mix can be changed, for example to meet changing customer needs.

- ☐ There are benefits and drawbacks of unlimited liability (more freedom, high risk, could lose everything) and of limited liability (more rules, less risk of losing home).

- ☐ A sole trader has certain characteristics - own boss, sets own targets, has unlimited liability, keeps the profits, can be risky.

- ☐ Private limited companies have different characteristics - shareholders, must file accounts, shares profits and decisions, limited liability limits risk for shareholders - can only lose what they put in.

- ☐ Establishing a unique trading or business name could be a USP for a business. The name must be memorable.

- ☐ Record keeping is important to help get tax payments right. .

- ☐ Tax responsibilities for a business can include VAT (not related to wages but to buying and selling), income tax (paid by the business on behalf of employees), National Insurance contributions (paid by both employees and employers) and corporation tax (paid by some larger companies on the profits they make).

- ☐ Repeat purchases can benefit a business as customers return to buy goods rather then buying from competitors.

- ☐ Businesses must recruit the right staff, in the right place, at the right time.

- ☐ Job adverts are used to encourage applicants for posts.

- ☐ A job description is an overview of the job, e.g. a cleaner wanted for a restaurant.

- ☐ Job particulars give more detail of the post, e.g hours of work, wages.

- ☐ A person specification includes the skills, qualities, attitudes and qualifications needed for a job, e.g. good communication skills, degree in Maths etc.

- ☐ The selection process involves letters of application, CV, short-listing and interviewing.

- ☐ Selection criteria includes a review of the candidate's skills and attitude and also whether they will fit in.

- ☐ Training can be on the job (in-house) or off the job (college, role play).

- ☐ There are laws affecting recruitment and selection, e.g. equality, minimum wage, health and safety.

- ☐ Employees can be motivated by giving them incentives and empowerment. A well motivated workforce is more likely to work hard and to keep labour turnover down.

Support activity

- Identify the 4Ps, with examples, from three local businesses using local newspapers, directories or using local knowledge.

- Identify three job adverts and try and get information on the job description and person specification for each job. Identify differences between the features of a job description and a person specification.

- Use your own experience to list the good and poor features of customer service.

Stretch activity

- Identify one example of an online shop and a traditional shop in the same market. Compare and contrast the customer experience of shopping online with traditional shopping. Which do you think offer the best level of customer service and why?

- Compare and contrast the marketing mix of two small or medium-sized local businesses.

- Identify three job adverts and try and obtain details of the job description and person specification for each. Write a short report evaluating the quality of the information included, where they were advertised and how useful they were to prospective applicants in providing appropriate information.

(a) Gabriel Ribeiro is setting up his own kitchen studio, Cozinha, in Manchester. He has put £20,000 of his own money into starting the business. Friends have invested another £40,000. The kitchens will be made indiviually to customer specifications and so Gabriel estimates most kitchens will be priced upwards of £10,000. Gabriel has been advised to make Cozinha a private limited company so he himself will have limited liability.

(i) What is meant by the term 'limited liability'? (1)

(ii) Explain why Gabriel was advised to make 'Cozinha' a private limited company rather than stay as a sole trader. (3)

Think: What is limited liability? What benefits? What drawbacks? What is in this scenario to use in the answer? Is there an alternative? Is it better or worse?

Student answer	Examiner comment	Build a better answer
(i) You're only liable for a limited amount.	■ Very weak answer rescued, just, by the addition of the word 'amount'. Has left a lot of doubt in the examiner's mind about actual understanding.	▲ Use clear phrases such as '… as a shareholder you can only lose the amount of money you invested, so your own possessions are safe.' Or use an example, such as 'you're only liable to lose the amount of money you put in, in Gabriel's case £20,000.'
(ii) Because he doesn't want to lose everything he owns.	■ A very basic comment which is correct but not developed.	▲ Identify one positive feature and its benefit but then link it to others. For example, 'Gabriel is dealing in expensive items so business might be infrequent. If the business failed then the maximum he could lose would be £20,000. This means his house and other possessions are safe, but it means not all the profit is his. This would be less of a risk than being a sole trader. ' Or identify an alternative and explain why that is not a good idea to get a similar answer. For example, 'As a sole trader he would be liable for all debts if the business had to close. This means he could risk losing his house, his car, in fact he could lose everything. By creating a private limited company he only risks losing what he invested (£20,000)'.

Practice Exam Questions

Sharon Kocabas was environmentally friendly. She sorted all her rubbish into different bags for recycling. It was time-consuming and Sharon wished it would happen automatically. Then the idea hit her to design a bin where you put the rubbish in the top, it read the bar code and sorted the rubbish into appropriate coloured bags via a rotating carousel. Refuse collectors simply picked up the bags and put them onto the wagons. Sharon realised this had potential with a USP, but needed to be marketed properly. She decided to call it BINSKA in order to get the idea across that it was a bin and it scanned. SCANBIN didn't sound right and using the K added a bit of class, she thought.

In creating her marketing mix Sharon focused on promotion to show how it worked. She felt the product spoke for itself, price would not be an issue at £149.99 and she would sell it through DIY outlets and to local councils. BINSKA would also supply the bags, which are recyclable, and took out a patent on them. Sharon got support from the bank, but it advised her to make BINSKA a private limited company to protect any investment. Sharon could not do it all by herself. She needed someone to look after the record-keeping such as VAT, National Insurance, tax and wages. She needed sales

staff to sell the product, but who also had detailed knowledge of the product to ensure customers were happy and would recommend her product to others. General office staff were needed to assist with the day-to-day running of the business. Sharon advertised for staff using a variety of adverts appropriate for the job. In order to keep staff motivated and to make them feel valued, Sharon introduced pay incentives and free health care.

(a) Which **two** of the following **best** describe Sharon's reason for offering free health care? She wants to:

A motivate the staff to work hard for her

B improve her record keeping

C meet customer needs

D promote the image of the product

E advertise for new staff

F keep staff from leaving (2)

(b) Explain how Sharon plans to deliver good customer service. (3)

(c) Evaluate Sharon's marketing mix for launching BINSKA. (8)

Topic 1.5: Understanding the economic context

Case study

Norford's is a small business that manufactures testing equipment. Its customers are other businesses that need to test the quality of their own products. For example, a crane manufacturing company might want to test the strength of a piece of steel when put under pressure. At what stress level will it snap? An aircraft manufacturer might want to test at what temperature - both high and low - a component might explode due to extreme heat or cold.

Topic overview

This topic considers the economic factors that affect businesses. How does the interaction of demand and supply affect the price charged and the quantity sold? How do changes in interest rates affect a business? How do changes in exchange rates affect exports and imports? What is the business cycle and how are businesses affected at different stages in the cycle? How are stakeholders affected by these factors?

Norford's operates in a market with only a small number of competitors. Like many businesses, it can set its own prices. However, this is very different from some of the firms from which it buys. Some of these suppliers have to accept the price that the market dictates. One example is suppliers who manufacture steel. Steel firms produce a commodity product. The price of steel is determined on international markets like the London Metal Exchange. Here buyers and sellers of steel from all over the world meet to agree trades, which set the price for steel. When demand for steel falls, even by a few per cent, there can be a large fall in the price of steel. Norford's uses a lot of steel in its products. Changes in steel prices can have a major effect on Norford's costs - either increasing them or cutting them.

Interest rates are another major cost that Norford's has to face. It has loans and an overdraft of £50,000. If interest rates fall, this can help cut the interest payments that the business has to make. If interest rates rise, the increase in costs can be damaging to the cash flow of the business.

Interest rates are likely to fall if the economy suffers a downturn. When this happens orders for equipment from Norford's can fall dramatically, as the customers it supplies cut back on their spending. The situation only gets better when consumer spending picks up again. Until that time firms will not feel confident about ordering new equipment; why should they if they do not think they will sell what they are producing?

One positive aspect of a downturn in the economy for Norford's is that the value of the pound is likely to fall. This makes its exports more price competitive. Without a fall in the exchange rate, the drop in orders could be even greater.

In a time of economic downturn, Norford's has some difficult decisions to make. It employs 11 workers. Should it make some workers redundant? If the firm is making a loss, the two owners of the business will not be able to take any profit out of the business. If this happens then Norford's has to investigate other ways in which it could cut costs. Could it squeeze its suppliers more by negotiating lower prices? Could it use the fall in the exchange rate to put up its prices to foreign customers?

1. How might Norford's be affected by each of the following?
   (a) There is a sharp cut in worldwide demand for oil.
   (b) The Bank of England decides to raise interest rates.
   (c) The value of the pound rises against the euro.
   (d) The economy goes into recession.

2. Who are the stakeholders in Norford's highlighted in the passage?

3. How might an increase in demand for testing equipment affect Norford's stakeholders?

What will I learn?

Market demand and supply How do the forces of demand and supply determine the price of goods in commodity markets? What are the differences between commodity markets and normal markets? What is the impact on small firms of price changes in raw materials and energy costs?

The impact of changes in interest rates on small businesses How do changes in interest rates affect small firms that tend to rely on overdrafts and loans for finance? What is the impact of changing interest rates on consumer spending?

Impact of changes in exchange rates What is meant by an 'exchange rate'? How do changes in the value of the pound against the dollar and the euro affect small firms that trade abroad or face competition from abroad? What impact do changing exchange rates have on the price of imported and exported goods? How can the prices of products be calculated using exchange rates?

How business cycles affect small businesses Why does the level of economic activity tend to rise and fall? How can changes in the level of economic activity affect small businesses?

The effect of business decisions on stakeholders What is meant by the term 'stakeholder? How do business decisions have different effects on different stakeholders? What are the problems that a business may face in meeting the demands of all stakeholders?

How will I be assessed?

Unit 1 A forty-five minute written examination of multiple choice and objective test questions.

Unit 2 Research and investigate a real life business from a choice of five tasks and write up the results under controlled assessment conditions.

Unit 6 A forty-five minute written examination of multiple choice, objective test and extended answer questions.

24 Demand and supply

Case Study

George Rixon owns a farm. For most of the past ten years, George has struggled to make a profit. This is the reason why he and his wife, Hannah, have diversified their business. 'Diversified' means they have done other things apart from growing crops and rearing animals. They started by opening their farm to school groups. Then they opened a tea shop to cater for the growing number of visitors. This year, Hannah will be opening a farm shop.

Objectives

- Understand that prices in commodity markets are determined by the balance between supply and demand.
- Appreciate the difference between commodity markets and normal markets.
- Understand the effect on small firms of price changes in raw materials and energy costs.

edexcel ::: key terms

Commodities – raw materials such as coal, oil, copper, iron ore, wheat and soya.

Commodity markets – where buyers and sellers meet to exchange commodities - often these are international, organised markets, for example the London Metal Exchange and the New York Mercantile Exchange.

Demand – the amount consumers are willing and able to buy at any given price.

Supply – the amount sellers are willing to offer for sale at any given price.

Shortage – when the demand for a good or service is greater than the supply. When a shortage exists, prices will tend to rise.

Surplus – when the demand for a good or service is less than the available supply. When a surplus exists, prices will tend to fall.

Demand and supply in commodity markets

Raw materials like copper, iron ore, coal, oil and wheat are called **commodities**. Farmers produce a range of commodities from wheat and potatoes to carrots, beef and milk.

Many commodities are traded on organised, global **commodity markets** where buyers (who represent the **demand** for a commodity) and sellers (who represent the **supply** of a commodity) come together to agree prices. Farmers like George, for example, send their wheat harvest off to market to be sold. The price they get is set by the balance between demand and supply.

Demand Demand for a product is the amount that buyers are willing and able to purchase at any given price. Wheat, for example, is used to make products such as bread, pasta, biscuits, beer, flour and animal feed. The demand for wheat is affected by the decisions of millions of businesses and individuals throughout the world who buy these products. If the demand for wheat rises, it will affect the price of wheat. Countries like China and Russia are major importers of wheat, buying wheat on world markets. China is a fast growing economy. With fast rising incomes, Chinese people are choosing to eat more food including more meat. This increases the demand for wheat because wheat is used for food and to feed animals.

Supply Supply for a product is the amount that sellers are willing and able to sell at any given price. The supply of wheat, for example, is just as affected by global conditions as the demand for wheat. There are hundreds of thousands of small farmers who produce wheat throughout the world. The supply of wheat depends partly upon the prices that farmers think they will get for wheat compared to other products they could grow. It also depends on weather conditions, pests and diseases, all of which affect the size of harvests. In 2007, for example, bad weather hit wheat harvests in Australia, parts of Canada, the United States and Europe with the result that the world supply of wheat fell.

If demand for a commodity is greater than supply, then there will be a shortage. Prices will rise when a **shortage** exists in a market. The bigger the shortage the greater will be the rise in price. In other situations, the supply of a commodity can be greater than the demand. In this situation, there will be a **surplus** and prices will fall.

Differences between markets

In recent years, the price of oil has changed very quickly - rising sharply in some periods but then falling back just as quickly. However, the price of most items in the shops does not change like this. There is a difference between commodity markets and the market for everyday goods and services that we all use, called **goods markets**.

Hannah Rixon, for example, will sell a packet of luxury biscuits in her farm shop at the same price over a period of time. The price of a cup of tea in her tea shop stays the same for at least 12 months. The price of most of what we buy in the shops changes only slowly. So what is the difference between the price of wheat and the price of a packet of biscuits?

Consumers like prices to stay the same. They find it confusing if prices are changing sharply week by week. For example, Hannah's tea shop customers would not like it if one week she charged 80p for a cup of tea and £1.50 the next week. Schools would not like it if they organised a visit to George's farm and found the entrance price had gone up by 50 per cent. So, businesses are under pressure to keep their prices the same. It can also be expensive for businesses to keep changing prices - the labels would have to be changed, for example.

George has less control over the price he gets for selling his wheat. He sends it to auction and gets what price he can for it. However, a biscuit manufacturer has much more control over prices. It can issue a list of prices for its products to customers like Hannah who wants to stock some luxury biscuit lines in her new shop. If sales are down one week, it can quickly stop producing or stockpile what it does not sell. In normal economic conditions, most businesses can fix the prices of the products they sell, at least in the short-term.

Changing commodity prices and planning

Businesses have little control over the price they have to pay for many of the raw materials they have to buy. The prices are determined on international markets. However, changes in the prices of commodities can affect small businesses significantly. In 2007 - 2008, the price of oil rose dramatically, from around $60 a barrel to $147 a barrel. By December 2008 the price of oil had fallen to under $50 again. The prices of commodities like wheat, beef, oil or copper change on a minute by minute and day by day basis. George Rixon can take his cattle to market one week and get a different price from the one he gets the next week when he takes more cattle to be sold.

With commodity prices changing so quickly, the plans of small businesses, such as cash flow forecasts, can be thrown into chaos. A plumber, for example, might find the cost of copper piping rising quickly because of global commodity price changes. Bakers may find wheat prices rising sharply. Builders may have to pay more for steel used in construction projects.

Raw material and energy costs

For many small businesses the largest single cost is paying wages to employees or paying yourself a wage. There are many other costs such as rent on premises, taxes payable to the government or new machinery.

Many small businesses also have to buy raw materials (commodities) and energy. George Rixon on his farm, for example, has to pay out for fertilizers, seeds and diesel. Hannah Rixon in her café has to pay electricity and gas bills for heating, lighting and cooking. If commodity prices change, it can have a major impact on the costs of production for small businesses. The size of the effect depends on three factors.

- What proportion of total costs are made up of raw materials and energy costs? Raw materials are a large proportion of the total costs for George Rixon on his farm. So changes in their prices have a big impact on his costs and his profit.

Watch Out!

Some firms are **price takers**. This means they cannot control the price they get for their production. Producers of commodities are price takers. Most firms, though, are **price makers**. They have some limited ability to set their own prices. However, price makers still face the harsh law of demand. The higher the price, the less it will sell. So price makers have to trade off higher sales for lower prices and vice versa.

Watch Out!

Remember that there is a difference between 'price' and 'cost'. Price is the amount of money that has to be handed over to acquire a good or service. Cost refers to the amount paid by producers to manufacture or produce a product or service, for example, for wages, raw materials, equipment and machinery, insurance, taxes and premises etc.

edexcel ⋮⋮⋮ key terms

Goods markets – the market for everyday products such as clothes, food, petrol, going to the cinema, a DVD etc.

118

These costs are a much smaller proportion of total cost for Hannah in her café and her new farm shop. So she is less affected.

- How large is the change in price? If commodity prices go up by 1 per cent, this will have little impact on many businesses, even those where they are a large proportion of total costs. If commodity prices go up by 50 per cent, this is likely to have a more significant impact on all businesses.
- Can the business pass on the increase in costs? If the price of fertilizer goes up by 50 per cent, George Rixon cannot pass on any of these extra costs to his customers. This is because he has no control over the price he gets for his products. He sells them at auction and has to accept whatever price is set. So some businesses have to **absorb** increases in costs. They have to pay them themselves. This reduces their profits and in some cases can even push a business into a loss. If the price of fuel, seeds and fertilizer rises but George gets a lower price for his wheat then it can force him to have to think about closing the business. Other businesses can **pass on**

increases in costs. This means they can increase their prices to reflect the higher prices they have paid for raw materials. In her café, Hannah Rixon can add 10p to a cup of tea if the price of electricity goes up. Businesses usually absorb small increases in costs in the short term. However, many businesses review and if necessary change their prices at least once a year to reflect changes in costs.

Ultimately, changes in costs of raw materials are important to a business because they have an impact on profit and survival. Rises in costs will lead to a fall in profits unless it can raise its prices or sell more of its products. If it cannot raise its prices or find a way of selling more products, the business could start making a loss. Ultimately, this could force it to close down.

Falls in costs, however, tend to make things easier for a business. It has to decide whether it can raise its profits by not passing on the cost reductions to customers. Or it could cut its own prices and hope that demand for its products will rise.

Test yourself

1. The price of oil rises on world markets. This is **most likely** to be because

   A the demand for oil has fallen
   B the supply of oil has risen
   C the supply of oil has risen faster than the demand for oil
   D the demand for oil has risen faster than the supply of oil

   Select **one** answer.

2. Jake Wooley runs a flower shop in London. He buys most of his flowers from a supplier in the Netherlands. The supplier in the Netherlands increases its prices. Jake's decision about whether he puts up the price of flowers to his customers because of this cost increase is **most likely** to depend on

   A how much insurance he pays
   B how big is the increase in the price of the flowers he buys
   C the amount of flowers he sells each week
   D which supplier he buys his flowers from
   E how large a proportion of his total costs is made up from buying flowers

   Select **two** answers.

3. Dylan Parkes has re-opened a former tin mine in Cornwall. He produces a small amount of tin which he sells at auction in London. He also uses the mine as a tourist attraction, charging visitors to come and see old workings. Which one of the following is **most likely** to be true about his business?

Select **one** answer.

A He has to accept whatever price is set at auction for his tin
B He has no control over the price he sets for visitors to see the mine
C He cannot charge a higher ticket price to visitors in July and August than at other times of the year
D He can decide for what price he sells his tin

Over to you

Gillams is a small firm that makes steel parts for machines. Over the past twelve months it has seen the price of steel double. Steel is a commodity that is traded on world markets. In recent years, the demand for steel from China and other fast growing economies has increased rapidly. The size of the Chinese economy is doubling every seven years. China's cities are seeing a construction boom and steel is in very heavy demand for new buildings.

Gillams has no choice but to pay the higher prices for steel. However, it is being hard hit by the price increases. Its customers are putting pressure on the company not to put up its prices. They are hinting that they will buy their parts from a different supplier if Gillams chooses to go ahead with a price rise. On the other hand, Gillams has worked closely with many of its customers for a number of years, giving excellent service. Competitors have also been putting up their prices. So Gillams has made the decision to raise its prices too by 10 per cent.

Otherwise, it faced making a loss and it could in the long term be forced to close.

1. Steel is a commodity. Its price is determined in international markets. Explain why the price of steel might rise on these markets. (3)
2. Analyse **two** possible effects on Gillam's if it had not increased its prices by 10 per cent. (6)
3. Evaluate how Gillam's customers might react to the 10 per cent increase in price. (6)
4. Discuss whether Gillam's workers have benefited from the 10 per cent price increase. (6)

ResultsPlus
Exam Question Report

15. Tina Dutton and Andrea Winders live in Warrington, Cheshire. Together they have set up a new business called Pink Ladies. Tina had wanted to set up her own business for some time but it was when talking to her daughter, Leanna, that she got the idea for Pink Ladies. Leanna had explained how she was often scared coming home at night in a taxi. Tina and Andrea did some market research and found that a surprising number of women were attacked in unlicensed taxis. Their business provides a taxi service for women only. The taxis are all painted pink and have pink interiors and are driven by women who have undergone training not only in driving but also in self-defence. The taxis all have satellite navigation and tracking devices. Customers pay to become members of the Pink Ladies Club and so the cars do not have cash with them. Customers receive text messages or phone calls to tell them where the taxi is and the driver does not leave until the customer is safely in their destination.

Which **two** of the following would be the most likely causes of a fall in demand for the Pink Ladies taxi service? (May 2008) (2)

A   A rise in the cost of buying the taxis
B   A rise in the local crime rate
C   A rise in unemployment in the Warrington area
D   A rise in the prices charged by other taxi firms in the Warrington area
E   A fall in interest rates
F   A rise in the exchange rate with the Euro
G   A reduction in the price of late night bus fares in the Warrington area
H   An upturn in the business cycle

Answer C and G

How students answered

Some students (32%) scored poorly (ie 0) on this question. These answers did not identify any factors that would have caused a **fall** in demand. They chose answers A, B, D, E and F, which were all likely to have caused a rise in demand for taxis or have little direct effect. For example, a **rise** in the local crime rate (B) could have persuaded women to use a taxi service particularly geared towards women, rather then walk, leading to a rise in demand for a taxi service. A rise in the exchange rate (F) is **not likely** to directly affect the demand for a taxi service in Warrington.

Most students (51%) gained good (ie 1) marks on this question. These answers identified one of the factors that would have caused a **fall** in demand. For example, a rise in unemployment in the Warrington area (C) could mean fewer people with jobs and less income. They may cut back on taxi rides and either walk or find cheaper alternatives.

Some students (17%) gained very good (ie 2) marks on this question.

These answers identified that both a rise in unemployment (C) and a reduction in the price of late night buses in Warrington (G) would lead to fall in demand. People often take taxis at night and cheaper bus fares may lead them to use an alternative form of transport and demand fewer taxi rides.

- It is good news for UK firms that use imported materials. The price of imports will fall. This means that the costs of these UK firms will fall. They can then choose to pass on those lower costs in lower prices to customers and probably gain sales. Or they can keep their prices the same and increase their profits.

Summary

To convert pounds to a foreign currency, multiply the amount of pounds by the rate.

For example, if you want to change £500 into dollars at a rate of £1 = $1.50, multiply 500 x 1.50 = $750.

To convert an amount in a foreign currency to pounds, divide by the rate. If you want to know how much 300 euro is in pounds when the exchange rate is £1 = 1.10 euro, divide 300 by 1.10. This then equals £272.73.

Test yourself

1. A small firm orders $6,000 worth of materials from a foreign supplier. If the exchange rate is £1 = $1.50, how much in £ will it have to pay for the order?

   A *£4,000*
   B *£6,000*
   C *£9,000*
   D *£10,000*

   Select **one** answer.

2. A UK firm sells furniture and kitchen products to customers in Europe and buys raw materials from Germany. The value of the £ (pound sterling) falls sharply against the euro.

   The fall in the value of the £ is most likely to mean that

   A *its sales to customers in Europe will fall*
   B *the cost of raw materials bought from Germany will fall*
   C *it will export more to customers in Europe*
   D *its total costs will fall*

   Select **one** answer.

3. The value of the pound (£) rises against other currencies. This is likely to

   A *increase exports of goods by UK firms*
   B *make UK firms less competitive in foreign markets*
   C *reduce imports of goods by UK firms*
   D *make UK firms more competitive in the domestic market against imports to the UK*

   Select **one** answer.

Over to you

Bishton's is a small food manufacturer based in Milton Keynes. It makes frozen foods that it sells worldwide. It buys some of its ingredients from abroad.

Over the past six months, the value of the pound has fallen against the euro and the dollar. For example, whereas six months ago, £1 would buy 1.30 euro, it now only buys 1.00 euro.

Bishton's has been pleased with the fall in the value of the pound. It is mounting an aggressive sales drive abroad to market its products. Lower prices are one of the key elements in this marketing initiative.

However, Bishton's costs have risen. In the short-term, this has affected profits because it takes time for overseas sales to increase. Profits have also been affected because it has not increased its prices to UK customers. It sells 30 per cent of its output in the UK, all to shops and other retail outlets in tourist centres in the UK.

1. Bishton's buys 13,000 euro worth of raw materials from France. Using the exchange rates mentioned in the passage, calculate the **difference** in price in pounds (£) that it paid six months ago compared to today. Show your workings. (3)
2. The price of a pack of biscuits that Bishton's sells is £1.50. Explain what has happened to the change in the amount that its French customers will have to pay if the value of the pound changes from £1 = 1.30 euro to £1 = 1.00 euro. Show your workings. (3)
3. Explain **two** reasons why Bishton's might be 'mounting an aggressive sales drive abroad'. (6)
4. Do you think the fall in the value of the pound will benefit Bishton's or harm the business? Justify your answer. (6)

ResultsPlus
Build Better Answers

Stephen Cleeves has a small business making models of racing cars and other famous vehicles. Most of his business is with collectors in Europe, particularly France and Italy, whose currency is the euro. He exports his products to these countries. Some of the materials he uses are imported from France.

Which **one** the following is **most likely** to be the result of a rise in the value of the pound from £1 = 1 euro to £1 = 1.20 euro for Stephen's business? Select **one** answer.

A Sales to collectors in Europe will rise
B The business would move premises
C The price of materials he uses in the models brought in from France will increase
D The price of his products to collectors in Europe will rise

Answer D

Technique guide: A good way to remember the effect of the change in exchange rates is the mnemonic SPICED.

Strong Pound - Imports Cheaper, Exports Dearer.

There is a number of choices available so first:

Think: What is meant by a rise in the value of the pound? How is this likely to affect exporters of goods from the UK, importers of materials to the UK, businesses in foreign countries, buyers in foreign countries?

Then: Dismiss the choices that appear wrong. That would be B - it is not likely that Stephen would move his premises because the value of the pound has risen.

Decide: You are left with A, C and D. You have narrowed down the options.

Go through these:

A is incorrect. If you remember the SPICED mnemonic, the price of Stephen's products to his European customers will rise as a result of a rise in the value of the pound. So the business is likely to sell less, not more.

C is incorrect. Again, use SPICED to help you here - the price of imported raw materials for Stephen will fall. So material prices from France will fall, not rise.

This leaves you with the correct answer of D. As the value of the pound rises, the price of exports to foreigners is likely to rise.

27 The impact of the business cycle

Case Study

Lily Moatt owns and runs a small car dealership. She sells second hand cars. Sales have been good for the past five years but this year they have fallen dramatically. It is because of the recession that has gripped the economy.

Objectives

● Understand that economic activity tends to rise and fall.
● Appreciate that changes in the level of economic activity can have serious effects on small businesses.

ResultsPlus
Watch Out!

Not every business suffers in a recession. In a recession, the government often increases its spending. So firms that supply the government might see their sales increase.

edexcel ⠿ key terms

Economic activity – the amount of buying and selling that takes place in a period of time.

The economy – the economic activity carried out by people and businesses in a country.

Economic growth – rises in the rate of economic activity in an economy. It is measured by calculating the value of sales in an economy over a period of time.

The Economy

Every day millions of people in the UK make decisions to buy goods and services. Businesses provide goods and services to final consumers and to customers who may be other businesses. The simple act of deciding whether to buy a chocolate bar from a local newsagent is just one example of what we call economic activity. **Economic activity** is the amount of buying and selling that takes place in a period of time.

The economy is the term used to refer to all the people and businesses in a country that engage in this buying and selling. Over time, the level of economic activity changes. Sometimes the amount of buying and selling rises. People may feel confident about their jobs, their incomes may be rising and they make decisions to spend money. They may choose to go out to the cinema more often, eat meals out, buy new furniture for their homes, go on holidays and so on. When this happens, we say the economy is expanding.

There are other times when people feel less confident about the future. There may be a lot of news about job losses; people may worry that they might lose their job and so decide to cut back spending and postpone decisions to make some types of purchase. For example, they may decide to do without a holiday abroad, decide to make do with the existing furniture they have rather than buy new and decide to go out to eat less each month. If this happens across the economy then the amount of buying and selling - economic activity - will fall.

Economic growth

Fifty years ago, very few people owned a car. Today, there is one car on the roads for nearly every two people who live in the UK. People over the past fifty years have become much better off. They can afford to buy more and better food. Homes are packed with electrical appliances, from fridges to washing machines to televisions and games consoles. People live longer because they live in better housing and because they receive better medical care from the National Health Service. The norm today is for teenagers to stay on in full time education to the age of 18 and one third go on to university or college.

The reason why people are better off is because there has been **economic growth** averaging around 2.5 per cent per year. This means that every year, on average, the economy produces 2.5 per cent more goods and services than it did in the previous year. The Office for National Statistics (ONS) collects and publishes information about the level of economic growth in the UK. If you look at a graph of economic growth it shows how economic activity has changed over time. In one year, economic growth may be 3.5%, in the next year, 2.9% in the next year, 2.5% and so on. It is important to remember that economic growth of 1% is slower than a rate of 2.0%, for example, but it is still 'growth'. What has changed is the **rate** of growth.

Lily Moatt's car dealership has done well in recent years from this economic growth. With people buying more cars each year, her sales have increased.

The business cycle

On average, production and incomes have gone up by 2.5 per cent over the last 50 years. However, in some years, it is more than this and in some years it is less. Over a period of time there tends to be a regular pattern to the level of economic activity. There might be a few years where economic activity is rising but then there are other years when the economy slows down. In some cases, this slowdown can be prolonged and this has a special name - recession. The tendency for economies to have different levels of economic activity is called the **business cycle**.

How businesses are affected by different stages in the business cycle

In some years there is a strong increase in the level of economic activity. The economy is growing strongly (called a period of 'boom'). People feel confident about the security of their jobs and they may be getting reasonable pay increases each year. In these sorts of conditions, firms like Lily Moatt's car dealership can do very well. Consumers feel confident enough to make decisions to buy large items, like cars or furniture. Many of these expensive items are bought on credit. So levels of borrowing are high too. All types of businesses might be doing well. Restaurants may find they are busy every night. Firms who offer leisure and entertainment may find they see sales rise. People may decide to extend their houses or decorate and so builders find their services are in demand. In turn, businesses which supply other businesses, like builders merchants, for example, may also see an increase in their sales.

Strong economic growth does not last forever. There will be other times when economic activity begins to slow down. This is sometimes called a 'slowdown' or a 'downturn'. In this sort of situation, consumer confidence begins to fall. Consumers become less willing to borrow money to buy large items like cars. Lily Moatt's sales may fall in a downturn. She may react by cutting her stock of cars. This means she buys fewer second hand cars from the car auction rooms to sell to her customers. She does not want to be stuck with lots of cars on her garage forecourt that are not selling. Also, she knows that she will have problems with finance and cash flow. Selling fewer cars means that money will not be coming into the business so frequently. So cutting the number of cars she buys is one way to reduce the amount of money flowing out of her business.

In a downturn different businesses will be affected in different ways. Businesses that sell 'essential' items like food might not see sales fall very much. Other firms such as restaurants or leisure providers who sell goods or services people see as 'luxuries' may see their sales fall quite dramatically.

If people are cutting back on spending then it tends to be the 'luxuries' that they cut back on first. They may decide that their home is all right as it is and does not need decorating or any new furniture. Firms that sell products such as paint, DIY items and furniture may see their sales fall sharply. In turn they order fewer supplies from manufacturers so these businesses also see their sales start to fall.

In some cases the slowdown can be quite severe. If confidence is so bad that many people throughout the economy are cutting back it can cause major problems. Businesses may see sales fall so far that they are forced to close down. If many businesses are closing down then people lose their jobs. They may find it hard to get other jobs and so they will have to cut back spending. Those who have jobs are

Businesses can do well when there is a strong increase in the level of economic activity

edexcel key terms

Business cycle – fluctuations in the level of economic activity over a period of time. Most economies experience times when economic activity is rising and others when economic activity is slowing.

lucky if they get a pay rise. Businesses who supply other businesses may also have to close because they have lost their main customers.

The slowdown can be so bad that the amount of goods and services produced in one time period can actually be less than that produced in the previous one - the economy shrinks in size. In this case, economic growth will actually be negative. For example, economic growth of -1.5% means that the economy produced 1.5% less than it did in the previous year. The ONS usually produce statistics for economic growth every quarter (there are four quarters to a year). If economic growth is negative for two successive quarters, then it is called a **recession**.

In a recession, businesses like Lily Moatt's are particularly hard hit. Buying a car is a major expense and in a recession people may simply feel they cannot afford to buy products that have a large price tag like a car. In a recession, Lily might see her sales fall by 50 per cent. Seeing her sales halve in size means that she may make a loss instead of a profit. She still has to pay rent on the premises. Her electricity and telephone bills are still very much the same. So, she cannot halve her costs to match the fall in her sales. The best she can do is reduce the number of cars she has for sale and make some of her workers redundant. Some businesses do not survive and are forced to close and this is more likely for some types of businesses in a recession.

ResultsPlus
Watch Out!

Do not confuse 'redundancy' with 'sacking'. In times when the economy is slowing, firms may look to reduce the size of its workforce. In this case it may look to make workers redundant. This is where a job ceases to exist anymore. Do not say that businesses will sack workers - sacking workers refers to a case where the employee has broken the terms of their contract in some way - possibly through some disciplinary matter such as stealing or assaulting a colleague.

edexcel ⠿ key terms

Recession – a situation when the level of economic growth is negative for two successive quarters.

Eventually, however, the economy begins to recover and return to positive growth. In a recovery, economic activity begins to rise. So too do consumers' incomes. Consumers feel more confident and are prepared to increase their spending again. In particular, they begin to increase their borrowing to buy items. This is good news for Lily Moatt's car dealership. She begins to sell more cars, although it may not be as many as when the economy was growing strongly. Rising sales helps her to return to profit, although the profit is small. The recovery from recession can take quite a long time.

Test yourself

1. Cremin's is an independent shop selling DVDs. It has decided to open a second store in a nearby area of London. Which **one** of the following is most likely to be the reason why it has decided to expand?

   A **Interest rates are at record high levels**
   B **The economy is growing very fast**
   C **Competition from Internet retailers of DVDs is getting more intense**
   D **Rents on shops are very high**

   Select **one** answer.

2. Agaba's is a restaurant. The economy is doing badly at the moment, incomes are falling and unemployment is rising. Agaba's has seen a drop in sales too. Which **one** of the following is most likely to help Agaba's survive?

   It should

   A **take on an extra worker**
   B **buy another local loss-making restaurant**
   C **introduce a take-away service**
   D **increase the pay of the owners of the restaurant**

   Select **one** answer.

3. Dineley's is a small taxi firm. It has decided to sell one of its taxis. Which **one** of the following is the most likely reason for this? Over the past twelve months

   A **the level of economic activity in the economy has fallen**
   B **the price of diesel has fallen**
   C **another local taxi firm has closed**
   D **the price of second hand cars has fallen**

   Select **one** answer.

131

Over to you

Gisborne's is a small firm which supplies spare parts for diggers used in construction and road building. It buys stocks from major manufacturers and then sells them to businesses that own diggers.

Twelve months ago, the firm was doing well and had achieved the highest sales ever in its four year history. It had expanded the number of parts it kept in stock to cope with higher sales and taken on an extra member of staff. It had also moved to larger premises, taking out a large loan to pay for the move.

However, recent months have been very bad for Gisborne's. The level of economic activity has fallen and the economy has gone into recession. As the business cycle has changed, economic growth has fallen by 2 per cent. The construction industry has been particularly badly affected with sales falling by 25 per cent. This means that there are now a lot of diggers lying idle in builder's yards that do not need any replacement parts. The only good thing is that construction companies have stopped buying new diggers. They have been making do with the diggers they already own. Older machines break down more frequently and so need more parts. Even so, Gisborne's has seen its sales fall by 20 per cent.

1. Explain what is meant by the business cycle. (3)
2. Explain the likely impact that the change in the level of economic activity over the past 12 months is having on Gisborne's. In your answer, analyse the likely impact on revenues, costs and profits. (6)
3. Explain how making a worker redundant might help Gisbourne's during a slowdown. (3)
4. Compare **two** different measures that Gisbourne's might take to survive the slowdown apart from making workers redundant. Discuss which one you think could be the most important in ensuring its survival. (9)

 ResultsPlus
Build Better Answers

The economy is growing strongly. Explain how this could affect a business. (3)

Think: What does growing strongly mean? What are the features of strong growth? How could strong growth affect businesses?

■ **Basic** Explains that a business could benefit as people have more money. 'Strong growth means people spend more and businesses profits will rise.' (1)

● **Good** Explains that in a growth period income is relatively high. (1) Businesses may benefit, as people are earning more and so will spend more on goods and services produced by businesses. (1)

▲ **Excellent** Explains that growth has certain features, many of which can benefit a business, although there can also be costs and challenges. For example, 'If the economy is growing strongly, incomes are relatively high and people are confident about the future. (1) High incomes and confidence lead to higher levels of spending by customers and decisions can be taken with reasonable certainty. (1) Businesses earn high revenues and profits as a result and may be able to expand, although the expansion may lead to issues, such as having to employ more staff and changing catalogues for new products.' (1)

What are controlled conditions?

There are different levels of control which apply to different parts of the CA.

- **Formal supervision (High level of control)** - the candidate must be in direct sight of the supervisor at all times. Use of resources and interaction with other candidates is tightly prescribed.

- **Informal supervision (Medium level of control)** - questions/tasks are outlined, the use of resources is not tightly prescribed and assessable outcomes may be informed by group work. Supervision is confined to (i) ensuring that the contributions of individual candidates are recorded accurately, and (ii) ensuring that plagiarism does not take place. The supervisor may provide limited guidance to candidates.

- **Limited supervision (Low level of control)** - requirements are clearly specified, but some work may be completed without direct supervision and will not contribute directly to assessable outcomes.

Source: QCA Guidelines.

There are **3** linked processes within the controlled assessment

Task setting

- This section is subject to **formal supervision (High level of control)**. The tasks are set by Edexcel at the start of each academic year. Centres are not permitted to make up their own titles or use a title from a previous series in a current session.

Task taking

This section falls into **2** parts.

Research which is subject to limited supervision (Low level of control).

- During the research period you may work outside the centre. Results can be recorded in writing or electronically.

- You can use the research during the writing up time.

- The teacher must inspect the research and be satisfied the research is your own work and that it does not contain inappropriate material such as a plan or model answer.

Writing up time which is subject to formal supervision (High level of control)

- All writing up time is subject to strict supervision.

- The write up will be your own work. You will get only one attempt - no drafts are allowed and no feedback can be offered by, or asked for from, a teacher.

- During the writing up time the teacher must keep a record of the writing up time - in a similar way to the records kept for any other formal assessment. The teacher needs to keep research folders secure so that students do not have access to them outside research time.

- Once the writing up time is completed the work will be collected in by the teacher who is responsible for keeping the work secure.

Task marking

- This section is carried out by the **teacher and is subject to informal supervision (Medium level of control)**.

- Once the controlled assessment write up is completed, it should be marked and kept secure. This includes both research and written up work.

The nature of the tasks set

There will **5** questions based on each of the sub sections of Unit 1 content set by Edexcel.

Examples of these types of tasks could be as follows.

Task 1

What are the most important qualities that an entrepreneur needs to possess, in order to start up and run a business successfully?

You could:

- Identify a local entrepreneur
- Research entrepreneurs (gather information/data)
- Design a questionnaire or set of questions to ask a local entrepreneur. Use a questionnaire, if entrepreneur does not visit the school or and interview, if entrepreneur does visit the school to explore the relevant qualities of the entrepreneur
- Collect useful information/data
- Present useful information/data
- Analyse the presented information/data
- Evaluate the task using your analysis.

Task 2

What is the most important way in which a business you have chosen competes with its rivals?

You could:

- Choose a local business that has at least one competitor in the locality
- Research the competing businesses (gather information/data)
- Collect useful information/data
- Present useful information/data
- Analyse the presented information/data
- Evaluate the task using your analysis and suggest improvements.

Task 3

What is the most important way in which a business you have chosen motivates its workers?

You could:

- Choose a local business and investigate its human resources management
- Research HR management policies/processes/techniques (gather information/data)
- Collect useful information/data
- Present useful information/data
- Analyse the presented information/data
- Evaluate the task using your analysis and suggest improvements.

Task 4

What is the most important element of the marketing mix to a business you have chosen?

You could:

- Investigate the marketing mix of a local business of your choice
- Research the marketing mix of the business (gather information/data)
- Collect useful information/data
- Present useful information/data
- Analyse the presented information/data
- Evaluate the task using your analysis and suggest improvements.

Task 5

To what extent have recent changes in interest rates affected the business you have chosen to investigate?

You could:

- Investigate how interest rate changes are affecting a local business of your choice
- Research interest changes and their impact (gather information/data)
- Collect useful information/data
- Present useful information/data
- Analyse the presented information/data
- Evaluate the task using your analysis.

Task 6

How have changes in commodity prices affected the costs and profits of a business you have chosen?

You could:

- Choose a local business that sells a commodity or relies heavily on one
- Investigate how commodity market price changes affecting a local business of your choice
- Research commodity market price changes and their impact (gather information/data)
- Collect useful information/data
- Present useful information/data
- Analyse the presented information/data
- Evaluate the task using your analysis.

Note that the bullet point list given in each case above is a suggestion only - there are other ways of tackling the question and this will depend on what access the centre has to businesses, where the centre is located, the school's facilities and resources and so on.

Source: tasks from EDEXCEL sample papers and guidance.

Evaluation

In the CA up to **8** marks will be given for evaluation.

Evaluation is the act of making a **judgement**. In making a judgement you say something about how important/significant/valuable/ something is. You will be expected to offer some support for your judgement which means using evidence to back up your judgement. For example:

'Manchester United is a more successful club than Newcastle United'. This is your judgement. What evidence is there to support this judgement?

The evidence is that

'Manchester United has won the Premier League title (or its equivalent) 17 times, the Champions League 3 times, the FA Cup 11 times, the League Cup twice and are the 2008 World Club Champions. Newcastle United on the other hand has only won the top division title 4 times (the last in 1927), never won the Champions' League, the FA Cup only 6 times and the Inter Cities Fairs Cup once - in 1969.'
Note that this is:
- An objective evaluation
- Answers a question about whether Manchester United is a **more successful** club, not whether it is a **better** club.

Your judgements, therefore, should be **objective** which means they require evidence to back them up, not **subjective** which is about often unsupported opinion. Only offer subjective comments if they can be backed up. For example, if you interview 20 people about the quality of a product from business X and 80% of your survey says the product is high quality in their opinion you can make a judgement that your survey would support the view that Business X provides a high quality product.

Does the evidence you collected and your interpretation of it support the task you investigated? In Business Studies examples of evaluation might be:
- do you think that the business will be successful - if so how successful - very, very successful, quite successful, reasonably successful, hardly successful at all?
- do you think that the business should raise its price - if so by how much and why?
- what are the most important characteristics of a successful entrepreneur?
- should the business take out a loan? Justify your answer.
- to what extent has limited liability helped the business - a great deal, quite a lot, hardly any way at all?
- how much do you think that interest rates affected the business - a significant amount, quite a lot, a reasonable amount or hardly at all?
- do you think that the business should set up as a franchise? If so why - what are the reasons and why are these reasons more important than the reasons for setting up as another type of business organisation?

- Do you think price is the most important element of the marketing mix?
- Has the business managed to retain staff? How well has it done this? Very well, quite well, not very well at all?
- How unique is the USP of the business? Totally unique, quite unique, not that unique at all? Can it be easily replicated?
- How much part has location played in the success of the business? A great deal, quite a lot, not much at all?
- To what extent did the business use market mapping before going ahead? A great deal, quite a lot, not much at all?
- The 'it depends' rule. The size of the effect/cause etc. will depend on a number of things. For example, The effect of a rise in price will depend on how big the price rise is, whether consumers are loyal to the business, what competitors do and so on.

To carry out evaluation you need two main elements.
- Criteria by which to make the judgement.
- Consideration of both sides of the argument.

The criteria are the benchmarks at which to look. For example, if you are asked 'should the business take out a loan', you could consider the 'it depends' rule. This gives you criteria such as: it depends on the:
- risk
- reason
- cost of repayments
- urgency
- size of the business
- amount of debt against money put in by the owners.

The second is the evidence you need to complete the evaluation. For example:
- one advantage of a loan might be that the business can get the money immediately
- one disadvantage of a loan might be that the cost of paying back could be high if interest rates are high.
You must then make a judgement.
- If the advantages outweigh the disadvantages you might decide that the business should take out the loan.
- If the disadvantages outweigh the advantages you might decide that the business should not take out the loan.

To really make the evaluation of high quality you need to use your research to try and place a value on the different possibilities/qualities/factors/causes/reasons etc. This is where your research and the quality of your research is really important.

Good practice in evaluation

- Always come to a decision. For example 'Given the evidence presented the business should not raise its price.'
- There are key words which will help - **'because'** is one.

These 'joining' words help support and explain the judgement. For example, the evidence showed the cash flow forecast was accurate **because** the actual figures matched up well.'

- Another useful phrase to support and consolidate the evaluation is '**which means that**'. For example, 'Helen Rogers now works only 4 days a week which means that the objectives were met and she was right to set up on her own.'
- Remember that although you are being asked for your opinion, it should be **objective** - based on the evidence. For example, 'After considering the evidence carefully, the advantages of becoming a franchise clearly outweigh the disadvantages for this business. In this case the business should consider becoming a franchisee rather than operating as an independent business.'
- Don't lose sight of the original task in evaluating the outcome. For example, if the task requires an investigation into whether taking out a franchise was a wise move then comments such as 'Yes, because there was no competition and the company provided the intial support' are fine but 'No, he should have gone on his own as sole trader' is irrelevant to the task. 'No, because he doesn't motivate his staff' is not. It may be true but it is not relevant to the task set.
- Be **rigorous** with the facts. For example, 'there is a feeling that the business might not last' lacks rigour and focus. It is too speculative.
- Above all keep a **balanced** view. By looking at all the elements, the positives and the negatives, the evaluation becomes a source of added value. Don't just assume that there must always be a positive outcome - sometimes the evidence tells you something different - go with the evidence.
- The sequence of events can help you to evaluate. For example, '**If** X happens …. **then** y occurs …. **this is because**… .'

Possible problems in evaluation

- Saying 'I think the business should get a franchise' is your judgement. On its own this personal/subjective comment is not of much value because it has nothing to back it up and so has limited validity.
- It is not about what you did. For example, 'I went to the bakery to collect the information because it was local' is simple narrative (story) of what happened. It is not evaluation; no **judgement** is made.
- Nor is evaluation about your participation. For example, 'I enjoyed doing the graphs because I am good at IT and I could make a good job of them' is an example of evaluation of process - what you did. This is not something that will be given credit in the assessment.
- Presenting an opposite view for the sake of it, whilst tempting, should be avoided. For example, 'all of the people surveyed agreed they got good customer

service from Goodall's Farm Shop (positive) but I think the place is rubbish (negative)' is not good evaluation. If your evidence told you all the people thought service was good then you have to accept what your evidence has told you rather than your own personal opinion which has no evidence to back it up.

- Be careful not to confuse conclusion with evaluation. Evaluative comments can be given throughout your answer. The conclusion will draw together your analysis and allow you to arrive at a judgement based on the evidence and which relates to the question.
- Recommendations are not the same as evaluation. Recommendations **emerge** from conclusions - to make them valid they must be supported with reasons. A recommendation is a judgement, remember.

Your guiding principle should be

What was the original task and ask the question - was the work produced fit for the purpose.

Mark schemes

The following highlights the mark scheme for evaluation and shows examples of marks that might be gained.

1-2 marks

At this level your judgements will be simple, using little objective evidence to support them. Phrases such as 'I think that is true because 20 people in my survey said so.'

3-4 marks

Judgements will be based on some supporting evidence, probably to support the question. Phrases such as 'The evidence from the survey shows that … and also that … This means that …'

5-6 marks

In this mark range you will be making clear conclusions and judgements using a range of the data collected to support these. You will have some balance to your answer to recognise that there are two sides to the story. There will be good balance to the conclusion. Phrases such as 'During the research the business stated that it did … However, some other research showed that … This would suggest that … because the other research included a greater number of people and was carried out over 3 years.'

7-8 marks

The top range will have in-depth evaluation of all the evidence collected and the analysis. The judgements and conclusions will be related closely to the task and use the evidence clearly and appropriately to support judgements and conclusions made in relation to the question. Balanced judgements will be made using phrases such as 'At this stage the research overall shows that … But it could be argued that … This would seem to suggest that … and However this depends on …'.

149

How analysis and evaluation fit together

In the sample assessment material (SAMs) the following question is given:

What is the most important qualities that an entrepreneur needs to possess in order to start up and run a business successfully?

The implication of this question is that there is a number of qualities that an entrepreneur needs to possess to get a business up and running. In your research you will need to identify what these might be in relation to the business/entrepreneur that you have chosen to investigate. Given the time that you have available for research and

writing up, the examiners would expect you to identify around 3 - 4 qualities.

The analysis will come in explaining **what** these qualities are - in relation to your entrepreneur - and **how** they help him/her to set up and run their business.

In each question the maximum number of factors/issues etc. that you might be expected to identify and explain is between 3 and 5 depending on the question and the context. You simply do not have time to do any more than 5 at most. Remember the examiners are more interested in you demonstrating the skills rather than how many factors you can identify.

Having identified and analysed the factors using the research you have gained, you will then have to arrive at a judgement in relation to the question. Which of the 3 or 4 qualities that you have identified and analysed do you think is the most important to get the business up and running successfully? Remember, there is no 'right' answer to this - your judgement needs to be supported by the evidence you have collected and the analysis you have given. If you think that determination is the most important quality - that is fine provided your analysis contains enough evidence to support your judgement.

The very fact that you are investigating a particular business means that your answer will be different from those of other people. If your friend is looking at another entrepreneur then his/her conclusion may be that leadership was the most important quality. The evidence in that case may have pointed to this conclusion.

Welcome to examzone

Revising for your exams can sometimes be a scary prospect. In this section of the book we'll take you through the best way of revising for your exams, step-by-step, to help you prepare as well you can.

Zone In!

Have you ever had that same feeling in any activity in your life when a challenging task feels easy, and you feel totally absorbed in the task, without worrying about all the other issues in your life? This is a feeling familiar to many athletes and performers, and is one that they strive hard to recreate in order to perform at their very best. It's a feeling of being 'in the zone'.

On the other hand, we all know what it feels like when our brains start running away with us in pressurised situations and can say lots of unhelpful things like 'I've always been bad at exams', or 'I know I am going to forget everything I thought I knew when I look at the exam paper'.

The good news is that 'being in the zone' can be achieved by taking some steps in advance of the exam. Here are our top tips on getting 'into the zone'.

UNDERSTAND IT

Understand the exam process and what revision you need to do. This will give you confidence but also help you to put things into proportion. These pages are a good place to find some starting pointers for performing well at exams.

DEAL WITH DISTRACTIONS

Think about the issues in your life that may interfere with revision. Write them all down. Then think about how you can deal with each so they don't affect your revision.

FRIENDS AND FAMILY

Make sure that they know when you want to revise and even share your revision plan with them. Help them to understand that you must not get distracted. Set aside quality time with them, when you aren't revising and when you aren't worrying about what you should be doing.

COMPARTMENTALISE

You might not be able to deal with all issues. For example, you may be worried about an ill friend, or just be afraid of the exam. In this case, you can employ a useful technique of putting all of these things into an imagined box in your mind at the start of your revision (or in the exam) and mentally locking it, then opening it again at the end of your revision session.

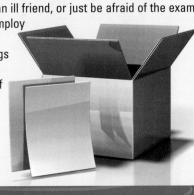

BUILD CONFIDENCE

Use your revision time not just to revise content, but to build your confidence for tackling the examination.

DIET AND EXERCISE

Make sure you eat well and exercise. If your body is not in the right state, how can your mind be?

More on the Active Teach CD

Planning Zone

The key to success in exams and revision often lies in the right planning. Knowing what you need to do and when you need to do it is your best path to a stress-free experience. Here are some top tips in creating a great personal revision plan.

First of all, know your strengths and weaknesses. Go through each topic making a list of how well you think you know the topic. Use your mock examination results and any further tests that are available to you as a check on your self-assessment. This will help you to plan your personal revision effectively by putting a little more time into your weaker areas. Importantly, make sure you do not just identify strengths and weaknesses in your knowledge of the content but also in terms of exam technique – what aspects of the assessment objectives are you weakest on, for example?

Next, create your plan!

Use the guidelines across the page to help you.

Finally, follow the plan!

You can use the sections in the following pages to kick-start your revision and for some great ideas for helping you to revise and remember key points.

More on the Active Teach CD

MAY

SUNDAY

29

MONDAY

TUES

Cut your revision down into smaller sections. This will make it more manageable and less daunting. In Business Studies you could follow the order of topics and sub-divisions within topics in the specification, which is clearly divided up already. Revise one at a time, but ensure you give more time to topics that you have identified weaknesses in.

Be realistic in how much time you can devote to your revision, but also make sure you put in enough time. Give yourself regular breaks or different activities to give your life some variance. Revision need not be a prison sentence.

Find out your exam dates. Go to www.edexcel.com to find all final exam dates, and check with your teacher.

Make sure you allow time for assessing progress against your initial self-assessment. Measuring progress will allow you to see and celebrate your improvement and these little victories will build your confidence for the final exam.

13

14

Make time for considering how topics interrelate. For example, in Business Studies, try to see where all the parts of the specification fit together. A business has to deal with lots of things all at once and cannot separate them out easily. You have to show that you are aware of all these factors. For example, a business might plan a marketing strategy but has to take into account the fact that interest rates might change and affect sales or that exchange rates may affect both costs and revenues if the business trades abroad.

Draw up a calendar or list of all the dates from when you can start your revision through to your exams.

Make sure that you know what the assessment objectives against which you will be measured are and what they mean. Get to know the command words that will give you a guide as to what assessment objectives you are expected to demonstrate.

27

28

Know Zone

In this section you'll find some useful suggestions about how to structure your revision for each of the main topics. You might want to skim-read this before starting your revision planning, to help you think about the best way to revise the content. Different people learn in different ways – some remember visually and therefore might want to think about using diagrams and other drawings for their revision. Others remember better through sound or through writing things out. Some people work best alone, whereas others work best when bouncing ideas off friends on the same course. Try to think about what works best for you by trialling a few methods for the first topic.

Remember that each part of the specification could be tested, so revise it all.

Writing revision plans

A useful technique to help you revise important points is to summarise topics into short points. It can be difficult to remember lots of information from textbooks or the notes you have taken during your course. To make notes on a topic:

● read the topic carefully;

● highlight the key points in the topic;

● identify the important information in each point;

● decide how to summarise each point into a short sentence so that it is easy to remember.

Below is an example of how this could be done for the topic 'forecasting cash flow' – which is part of Topic 1.3, Unit 1 – Introduction to Small Business.

Topic 1.3, Unit 1: Forecasting cash flows - Revision points

● Cash is notes and coins and money in the bank.

● Cash flow is the flow of money into and out of a business.

● Inflows (receipts) are cash coming into the business from owners, loans or cash from sales.

● Outflows (payments) are cash leaving the business to pay for wages, equipment, bills and materials.

● Net cash flow is calculated by inflows minus outflows.

● If inflows are greater than outflows, net cash flow in positive. If inflows are less than outflows, net cash flow is negative.

● A negative net cash flow can be a problem as less money is coming into the business than is going out.

● Without cash, a business may no longer be able to pay its debts and may become insolvent.

● A cash flow forecast is a prediction of how cash will flow through a business in a period of time in future.

● The opening balance in a cash flow forecast is the cash a business has at the start of a month or other period.

● The closing balance in a cash flow forecast is the cash a business has at the end of a month or other period.

● The closing balance shows the cumulative cash flow of a business.

● The opening balance plus the net cash flow equals closing balance.

● The closing balance in one month or other period becomes the opening balance in the next.

● If a business has a negative closing balance it will have a cash flow problem. It must avoid this by raising sales revenue, reducing costs or putting money into the business from an owner or from a loan.

● Selling more goods brings cash into the business.

● Cutting the cost of production reduces the cash going out of the business.

● Paying suppliers later for materials using trade credit reduces the cash going out of the business immediately.

● Payments using cash by customers increases the cash coming into the business immediately.

● Buying less stock reduces the cash going out of the business.

● Careful planning is needed to avoid cash flow problems before they occur.

It might also be helpful to make short notes on the type of question that could be asked in this area of the course and write down helpful tips in answering these questions. Across the page is an example of how this could be done for the topic 'Forecasting cash flows' – which is part of Unit 1 – Introduction to Small Business.

Topic 1.3, Unit 1: Forecasting cash flows – Important tips

In an examination, questions ask students to make calculations in a cash flow forecast by filling in gaps. Use the following formulae.

● Total receipts are found by adding up all the inflows of cash to the business.

● Total payments are found by adding up all the outflows of cash to the business.

● Net cash flow = inflows – outflows.

● Opening balance = closing balance from last period.

● Closing balance = opening balance + net cash flow.

I could be asked to comment on the cash flow position of businesses, state what problems/issues arise and explain how a business might be able to deal with the situation it faces. I must take into account the scenario given in the question. For example, a sole trader cannot bring more money in by selling more shares as there are no shares in a sole trader business.

Memory tips

In the examination you will need to remember important facts, information and data that will help you to answer questions. Some of these will simply be a list of terms, such as:

● the names of sources of short-term finance of a start up business;

● the stakeholders of a business;

● the methods of primary or secondary market research.

Others might be a list of phrases, such as:

● the main sources of added value;

● the advantages and disadvantages of a franchise in starting up a business;

● the qualities shown by entrepreneurs when starting up a business.

Different people remember in different ways. You might use some of the following methods to help you.

Memory tips – Mnemonics

This is a word that is made up from the first letters of the terms you want to remember. Some well-known mnemonics in business studies are:

● PESTLE – the Political, Economic, Social, Technological, Legal and Environmental factors affecting a business;

● SWOT – the Strengths, Weaknesses, Opportunities and Threats facing a business;

● the 4 Ps of the marketing mix – Price, Product, Promotion and Place.

You can make up your own mnemonic for a topic. For example, you might want to remember the main sources of added value as BUSCQD – Branding, Unique selling point, Speed, Convenience, Quality, Design (thinking about a bus queue and calling it Bus-ce-qued).

You can make-up mnemonics to help with explanation. For example, SPICED helps you to remember the effect of changes in the exchange rate:

Strong Pound – Imports Cheaper, Exports Dearer.

More on the Active Teach CD

Know Zone

Memory tips – Visual presentation

Some people remember if the information is a picture or diagram. Examples of diagrams that could be used include the following.

▶ A diagram to show the relationship between costs.

Variable costs = £8,000
(output of 1,000 X cost per unit of £8)

Total costs = £10,000

Fixed costs = £2,000

▶ A diagram to show objectives when starting a business. ▶ A diagram to show the stages in recruitment.

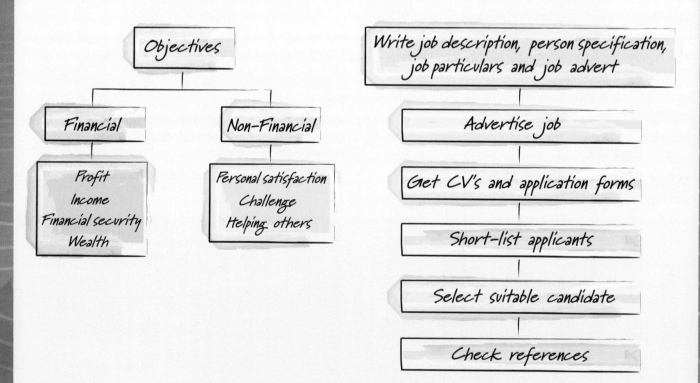

Objectives

Financial

Profit
Income
Financial security
Wealth

Non-Financial

Personal satisfaction
Challenge
Helping others

Write job description, person specification, job particulars and job advert

Advertise job

Get CV's and application forms

Short-list applicants

Select suitable candidate

Check references

Memory tips - Mindmaps

A mindmap is a diagram that records words and ideas and shows connections. At the centre of the map, or page, is the main word or idea. Flowing out from this main word or idea is a number of key words and ideas linked to the main word. Mindmaps are used in business as explained in section 12 of this book. But you can use a mindmap for your revision. Below is a simple mindmap outlining the Qualities shown by entrepreneurs.

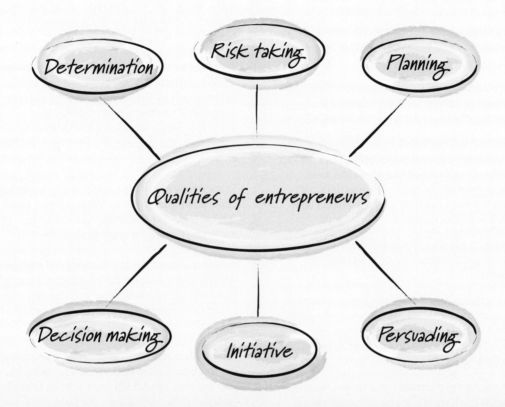

Don't Panic Zone

Once you have completed your revision in your plan, you'll be coming closer and closer to The Big Day. Many students find this the most stressful time and tend to go into panic-mode, either working long hours without really giving their brain a chance to absorb information, or giving up and staring blankly at the wall. Some top tips are shown here.

◉ Test yourself by relating your knowledge to business issues that arise in the news – can you explain what is happening in these issues and why?

◉ Get hold of past papers and the mark schemes for the papers. Look carefully at what the mark schemes are expecting of the candidate in relation to the question.

◉ Get hold of a copy of the Examiner's Report from the previous exam series. It contains lots of useful advice about where candidates performed well and where the main mistakes were. Learn from these. The Examiner's Report and past papers are often available on the awarding body Website – check with your teacher.

◉ Do plenty of practice papers to hone your technique, help manage your time and build confidence in dealing with different questions.

◉ Relax the night before your exam – last minute revision for several hours rarely has much additional benefit. A runner doing a marathon is unlikely to practice the night before by going for a quick 15 mile run. Your brain needs to be rested and relaxed to perform at its best.

◉ Remember the purpose of the exam – it is for you to show the examiner what you have learnt and understood about business. It is not a means of trying to trick you.

Last minute learning tips for Business Studies

The week before the exam should be spent going through past papers. Look at each question carefully and compare question types. Make sure that you are familiar with the different types of question and you know the style needed to answer each question.

There will be **multi choice** questions or **objective test** questions. These ask you to make a choice from a series of options, such as 'Which **two** of the following are the **most important** in spotting a new business opportunity?' or 'Which of the following is a reason why customer service is so important to the success of a small business? Select **one** answer.'

There will be questions assessing your **knowledge** and **application** skills, such as 'What is meant by the term "stakeholder"?' and 'Identify **two** examples of secondary market research data in the passage.'

Certain questions will test **analysis** and **evaluation** such as 'Explain how a hierarchical structure in a business might make communication more difficult' and 'To what extent can a business be ethically responsible and profitable? Justify your answer.'

Try to devote some time to actually writing out the answers in the time period allowed to refine your skills. You can check your answers against the mark scheme to see how you would have performed. Make sure you understand what the command words are for each question and how they relate to the assessment objectives. For example, an 8 mark question might consist of 2 marks for knowledge, 2 for application and 4 for analysis and evaluation.

Remember that you can get full marks by answering in the space provided on the exam paper - it is not the amount you write but the quality and the extent to which you demonstrate the assessment objectives being targeted.

On the night before the exam, relax, give your brain a rest and try and do something you enjoy. Get to bed at a reasonable hour so that you can get a good night's sleep and be refreshed for the exam.

More on the Active Teach CD

Exam Zone

About the exam paper

You'll notice a few different types of question on the examination paper.

For Unit 1 This is an external examination made up of compulsory multiple choice and objective test questions with a total of 40 marks. You will be given 45 minutes to answer these questions.

For Unit 2 This is an internally assessed task which is researched over a maximum of 6 hours and written up in controlled conditions in a maximum of 3 hours. More guidance on unit 2 assessment is given earlier in this book.

For Unit 6 This is an external examination made up of compulsory multiple choice, objective test and extended answer questions with a total of 40 marks. You will be given 45 minutes to answers these questions.

Understanding the language of the exam paper

Which of the following is... Select one answer	You need to identify the correct response from a selection of options.
Which two of the following are...	You need to identify the two correct responses from a selection of options.
Which of the following is most likely to...	The key is 'most likely' – this means that there could be more than one option that is possible; you have to decide which is the most likely.
Which of the following is not...	This is a question asking you to spot the negative option from a list – read each option carefully.
Fill in the blanks	This may require you to complete some calculations in a table, for example.
What is meant by...	This requires you to give a definition of a key term in business studies – an example to help support the definition is usually worth giving also.
Identify...	This type of question requires only a one word answer or a short phrase or sentence – it is associated with knowledge and understanding and often requires the student to extract information from a context.
State...	Similar to 'identify' – again usually only requires a one word answer.
Describe...	Give the main characteristics of a topic or issue.
Explain...	Describe the issue, term etc, giving reasons or features.
Analyse...	Break down the topic or issue into manageable parts to help explain what is going on, how something works, what relationships may exist and what assumptions might be made.
Assess...	Offer a judgement on the importance, significance, relevance and value of something, with reasons why you have made such a judgement.
Do you think...	Asking you to make a judgement – which requires support and reasons to be given for the judgement.
What is the most important...	Another question asking you to make a judgement and offer support for the judgement. Explain why one factor is more important than another and why.
To what extent...	Is the issue very, very important/significant/, quite important/significant, moderately important/significant, not very significant/important at all – and why?
Evaluate...	Arrive at a judgement – with some support for your reasoning.
Justify...	Offer support and reasons for the judgement you have made – and why.
Write a report...	A report might consist of advantages and disadvantages, key features, summaries and judgements about the value of one option against others.

Exam Zone

Meet the exam paper

This diagram shows the front cover of the exam paper. These instructions, information and advice will always appear on the front of the paper. It is worth reading it carefully now. Check you understand it. Now is a good opportunity to ask your teacher about anything you are not sure of here.

Print your surname here, and your initial afterwards and sign the paper. This is an additional safeguard to ensure that the exam board awards the marks to the right candidate.

Here will be the school's centre number.

Ensure that you understand exactly how long the examination will last, and plan your time accordingly.

Make sure you are aware of how many marks are given for each question and write to justify these marks.

Here you fill in your personal exam number. Take care when writing it down because the number is important to the exam board when writing your score.

In this box, the examiner will write the total marks you have achieved in the exam paper.

Make sure you understand what you are allowed to take into the exam and what you are not.

Make sure that you understand exactly which questions you should attempt and the style you should use to answer them.

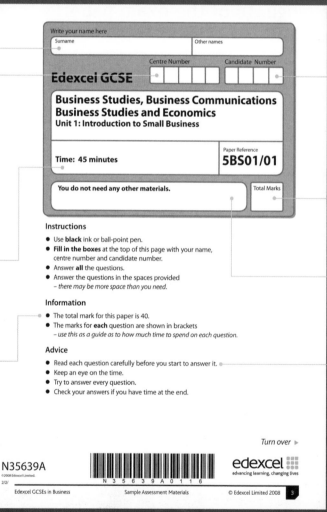

Write your name here

Surname

Other names

Centre Number   Candidate Number

Edexcel GCSE

Business Studies, Business Communications
Business Studies and Economics
Unit 1: Introduction to Small Business

Time: 45 minutes

Paper Reference
5BS01/01

You do not need any other materials.

Total Marks

Instructions

● Use **black** ink or ball-point pen.
● **Fill in the boxes** at the top of this page with your name, centre number and candidate number.
● Answer **all** the questions.
● Answer the questions in the spaces provided
  – *there may be more space than you need.*

Information

● The total mark for this paper is 40.
● The marks for **each** question are shown in brackets
  – *use this as a guide as to how much time to spend on each question.*

Advice

● Read each question carefully before you start to answer it.
● Keep an eye on the time.
● Try to answer every question.
● Check your answers if you have time at the end.

Turn over ▶

N35639A
©2008 Edexcel Limited.
2/2/

Edexcel GCSEs in Business   Sample Assessment Materials   © Edexcel Limited 2008   3

edexcel
advancing learning, changing lives

More on the Active Teach CD

Zone Out

This section provides answers to the most common questions students have about what happens after they complete their exams. For much more information, visit www.examzone.co.uk

About your grades

Whether you've done better than, worse than or just as you expected, your grades are the final measure of your performance on your course and in the exams. On this page we explain some of the information that appears on your results slip and tell you what to do if you think something is wrong. We answer the most popular questions about grades and look at some of the options facing you.

When will my results be published?

Results for summer examinations are issued on the middle two Thursdays in August, with GCE first and GCSE second.

Can I get my results online?

Visit www.resultsplusdirect.co.uk, where you will find detailed student results information including the 'Edexcel Gradeometer' which demonstrates how close you were to the nearest grade boundary. Students can only gain their results online if their centre gives them permission to do so.

I haven't done as well as I expected. What can I do now?

First of all, talk to your subject teacher. After all the teaching that you have had, tests and internal examinations, he/she is the person who best knows what grade you are capable of achieving. Take your results slip to your subject teacher, and go through the information on it in detail. If you both think that there is something wrong with the result, the school or college can apply to see your completed examination paper and then, if necessary, ask for a re-mark immediately. The original mark can be confirmed or lowered, as well as raised, as a result of a re-mark.

How do my grades compare with those of everybody else who sat this exam?

You can compare your results with those of others in the UK who have completed the same examination using the information on our website at: http://www.edexcel.com

What happens if I was ill over the period of my examinations?

If you become ill before or during the examination period you are eligible for special consideration. This also applies if you have been affected by an accident, bereavement or serious disturbance during an examination.

If my school has requested special consideration for me, is this shown on my Statement of Results?

If your school has requested special consideration for you, it is not shown on your results slip, but it will be shown on a subject mark report that is sent to your school or college. If you want to know whether special consideration was requested for you, you should ask your Examinations Officer.

Can I have a re-mark of my examination paper?

Yes, this is possible, but remember that only your school or college can apply for a re-mark, not you or your parents/carers. First of all, you should consider carefully whether or not to ask your school or college to make a request for a re-mark. You should remember that very few re-marks result in a change to a grade - not because Edexcel is embarrassed that a change of marks has been made, but simply because a re-mark request has shown that the original marking was accurate.

Check the closing date for remarking requests with your Examinations Officer.

When I asked for a re-mark of my paper, my subject grade went down. What can I do?

There is no guarantee that your grades will go up if your papers are remarked. They can also go down or stay the same. After a re-mark, the only way to improve your grade is to take the examination again. Your school or college Examinations Officer can tell you when you can do that.

Can I resit a unit?

If you are sitting your exams from 2014 onwards, you will be sitting all your exams together at the end of your course. Make sure you know in which order you are sitting the exams, and prepare for each accordingly – check with your teacher if you're not sure. They are likely to be about a week apart, so make sure you allow plenty of revision time for each before your first exam.

For much more information, visit www.examzone.co.uk

More on the Active Teach CD

Index

Page references which appear in colour are defined in the Key Terms sections in each subtopic.